Golden Secrets
of
Mystic Oils

by

Anna Riva

D1591048

Author of

Prayer Book
Power of the Psalms
Candle Burning Magic
Devotions to The Saints
Secrets of Magical Seals
The Modern Herbal Spellbook
Modern Witchcraft Spellbook
Golden Secrets of Mystic Oils
Magic With Incense and Powders
Spellcraft, Hexcraft & Witchcraft
Voodoo Handbook of Cult Secrets
Your Lucky Number ... Forever
How to Conduct a Seance

www.indioproducts.com

INTERNATIONAL IMPORTS
236 W. MANCHESTER AVE.,
LOS ANGELES, CA 90003

Occult Books - Curios - Supplies

Copyright © 1990
Reprint 2000

ISBN 0-943-83216-0

TEN COMMANDMENTS FOR A HAPPY LIFE

1   Today I will be grateful for all the things I have. I will not be envious of others who seem to have more material goods than I have.

2   Today I will not get angry nor concern myself with unimportant trifles.

3   Today I will not let the wrongdoing of others cause me to do wrong.

4   Today I will not be proud and look down on others.

5   Today I will not criticize others, nor find fault. I will speak softly, be considerate of others, and will dress neatly and look as well as I can.

6   Today I will do a good thing for someone else. It must not be something for which I expect anything in return.

7   Today I will keep busy and do work if I am in good health. I will not be lazy nor idle, though I will try to find a quiet hour for my own self.

8   Today I will be the best I can be. I will be sincere in my thoughts and gracious in my relations with others.

9   Today I will live for today. Yesterday is gone, and tomorrow may not come.

10 Today I will truly try to like all those with whom I come in contact.

ANNA RIVA

The Uses of Oils

The use of oily, fragrant materials to anoint the body is a custom going back to remote antiquity, evidenced in the Old Testament as well as other early books. The ceremonial and sacred use of oils was of early origin among the Hebrews and continues today in Christian rites of baptism and extreme unction. It has long been believed that odors have a curious effect upon mankind, both natural and supernatural. Magicians of ancient times anointed their bodies with oils that drugged their senses and induced visions. The use of divine oils is a primary way of getting in touch with the supernatural, and the use of odors as psychological stimulants is well established. Certain perfumes can act as aphrodisiacs. Various persons are sensitive to different fragrances, and there are many ways to employ oils for magical objectives.

DRESSING CANDLES

It is much preferred that one anoint or "dress" their own candles, rather than purchasing those which have been dressed by others, for it is believed that the close contact of the hands on the candle bring to it the thoughts which are foremost in one's mind. Concentrate on the purpose of the ritual and magnetize the candle with your belief and your faith as you anoint it with the appropriate oil.

A candle is dressed by rubbing the oil over its surface, beginning in the middle and applying toward each end, not in one stroke from top to bottom or bottom to top. From the middle upward, then from the middle downward until the entire outer surface is covered with the oil.

ANOINTING SEALS

To heighten and intensify the powers of symbolic seals, many persons consecrate them with an oil which has been chosen as applicable to the purpose toward which they are working. Unless specific or different instructions are given for a particular ritual, here is the most generally accepted way to magnetize the seal.

First moisten the fingertips with the oil to be used and place a dot of it at each corner of a square seal. Start at the top left, then bottom right, bottom left, and top right. Then connect the corners by beginning at the upper right corner and moving the finger downwards and around the seal, ending as you reach the top right corner again.

On a circular seal, apply four dots of oil, in sequence, to the north, south, east, and west points at the outer edge of the paper, skin or whatever material the seal is made of. Then connect the dots, beginning at the north, going in a counter clockwise direction, and ending back at the north point, completing the circle.

Usually, the consecration is repeated once a week unless other instructions are given in the suggested ritual.

ANOINTING CHARMS

To consecrate or magnetize any lucky charms or talisman, apply an appropriate oil to the outer edges once a week.

ANOINTING OBJECTS

For incense burners, tools, altars, or any irregularly shaped materials, use the oil in an imaginary triangle. When consecrating the implement for purposes of attracting, holding onto something, drawing vibrations inward, rub the oil in this imaginary triangle with its wide base away from you. Start at each end of the wide base and rub downward and inward along the sides of the triangle — always inward, always toward you, not in an up and down motion.

If you are anointing for the purpose of discarding bad influences, dispelling evil, or getting rid of troubles, begin the anointing at the tip of the triangle near you, rubbing upward and outward toward the wide base of the triangle — always upward and outward, away from you.

ATTRACTING,
DRAWING,
INVITING

REPELLING,
REJECTING,
DISPERSING

ANOINTING THE BODY

When applying oil to the body, unless specific instructions are given to the contrary, keep the imaginary triangle in mind. Think of your body as two triangles — upper and lower. The upper triangle would consist of the broad base across the chest area with the tip of it at the middle of the forehead. The lower triangle would consist of the broad base across the stomach with the tip at the feet placed close together.

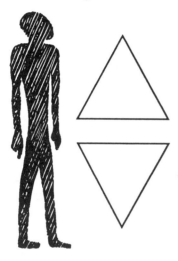

From this illustration, you should be able to decide the most appropriate way to anoint yourself — or another person — to accomplish the most from the procedure.

For instance, if you were depressed and attempting to rid yourself of this harmful feeling, the anointing would begin with rubbing the appropriate oil across the chest and upward over the shoulders, onto the side of the neck, over the cheeks, ending with the hands at the middle of the forehead.

On the other hand, if you are attempting a spell aimed at enticing a lover or attracting favors from others, begin the anointing with the hands at the middle of the forehead, bringing them downwards over the cheeks, neck, and shoulders, then across the body, meeting in the center of the chest.

For the lower portion of the body, such as ridding one of unhealthy sexual aberrations or keeping yourself away from undesirable associations, start by rubbing the oil across the stomach from the navel outward, then over the hips and down the outside of the legs, ending at the two big toes of the feet.

In attempting to pull favorable influences into the body, reverse the triangle — beginning with anointing the feet, bringing the movement up the legs, over the hips, and then into the body, ending near the center of the stomach area.

Keep in mind always the triangle which can be used on any part of the body. To bring money into the hands, for instance, start at the finger tips, coming up on each side of the hand and then across the wrists. Or, to get rid of pain in that area or to help one keep hands off a situation, reverse the process, beginning it across the wrists and away from the body, ending at the tip of the middle finger.

The most important points to remember in anointing is inward motion for attracting, outward motion for repelling — and always in one direction only, never an up and down or backward and forward stroke.

OTHER USES

A bottle of oil can simply be kept open in a room to entice or repel those particular influences for which it was formulated.

Oils are sometimes poured or sprinkled in the bath, on dolls or images. They are added to incenses and scrub waters. They are worn as perfumes and sprinkled on clothes as a deodorizer.

This book contains over 1300 uses of oils, but there are countless other spells and rituals which involve occult and psychic oils. If the reader has the interest, experiment — change and modify the spells to suit your particular and special purpose. For it is your mental energy and the power of your subconscious mind which is the only true magic.

Mystic & Occult Oils

In this A to Z list you will find over 550 of the most popular oils which are widely available from occult supply houses. Certainly if you read through the various uses for these oils, you will find one or more which is formulated to help you solve the problem, do the job or assist you with the situation you are facing.

Names of oils are those given them by the maker, and does not indicate that any claims of supernatural powers are made or intended. No attempt has been made to list every brand name given to the oils by manufacturers or dealers. Duplication, or closely similar names, have been omitted — for instance, Double Cross Oil is listed, but XX Double Cross and XXX Double Cross are not. Success Oil is listed, but Crown of Success is not. Protection Oil is listed, but Special Protection is omitted because its uses and attributes are closely related to those given for Protection Oil. Such names as Oil of Life, Oil of Mars, and Oil of Q are listed under Life, Mars, "Q", etc.

No effort has been made to distinguish between oils, essences, and perfumes. In the occult use, there is no difference in the uses of these three products. Generally, the difference in terms is one of strength — many oils sold are pure, undiluted fragrances, while essences are concentrated but have an aldehyde added to dilute the oil. Perfumes are basically the same as oils, but with more aldehyde or alcohol included than essences. Colognes are also similar, but weaker in content, and generally are not as long lasting. Colognes are not popular for occult use.

There are over 1,300 spells given in this book but there are so many others which could be included. No attempt has been made to give exact instructions, for the user should choose his own methods of use. In many spells, suggestions of "apply to the body," "anoint the candle," or "add to incense" is given — because this method is the one which has been used or proved successful for the author. But, unless specific warning of how NOT to use the oil, the reader can — and should — experiment with the spell to find the most convenient way to achieve the desired results.

ABRA MELIN — Cast a spell upon the person you wish to obey your wishes by writing your request on the reverse of a Seal of Aziabelis from the Sixth & Seventh Books of Moses. If the desire is for a beneficial purpose, use the Dove's Blood Ink, but if it is your aim to harm, then the Dragon's Blood Ink would be more appropriate. Anoint each corner of the talisman with oil as you chant with each drop:

> Do my bidding, I demand,
> Follow quickly what I say.
> This is my firm command.
> Obey at once, or rue the day.

ABSINTHE — This is a hexing oil used on one's enemies. Do not use it in your own home, but apply it to the body of a foe secretly so that the harm they have done to others will be drawn back unto themselves.

AC/DC — The formula for this is a closely guarded secret by those who know it, but a few occult shops do carry it. While it obviously has connotations of heterosexual and homosexual love variations, it can be used by anyone who is facing a decision of choice. Apply to the forehead just before going to sleep, and by the morning a dream or vision may help you decide which way to move in your situation.

ACACIA — See Exodus, Chapters 25, 26 and 27, where the Lord spoke to Moses and asked that the children of Israel bring material for the Tabernacle. Among the offerings of gold, fine-twined linen, olive oil, onyx stones, etc., was acacia wood. In the King James Bible the translation of acacia is given as "shittim wood." In The Living Bible, a modern translation which makes the Bible truly readable and easy to understand, the instructions from the Lord specified that the sacred Temple was to include an ark 3¾ feet long, 2¼ feet wide, and 2¼ feet high using acacia wood. The poles were to be of acacia overlaid with gold. A table 3 feet long, 1½ feet wide, and 2¼ feet high was to be of acacia. The framework of the sacred tent "shall be made from acacia wood, each frame-piece being 15 feet high and 2¼ feet wide." Finally, God, specified, "Using acacia wood, make a square alter 7½ feet wide, and 3 feet high."

Use this holy oil to anoint altars, altar cloths, incense burners, and candles. Use it on the body anytime you enter the church, a holy place, or when you pray before your home altar.

ADAM & EVE — Used by both sexes as a love oil to heighten the passions and to bind together lovers who have quarreled or grown apart.

AFRICAN JU JU — Same as Ju Ju Oil, an attracting and protective agent. See uses under Ju Ju.

ALGIERS — From this melting pot on the Mediterranean Sea comes an intriguing fragrance which brings a mysterious allure wherever it is used.

Apply it to a light bulb (before it is turned on, never when the bulb is already heated) for a sensuous setting that stimulates the tender feelings of the heart for all those in the room.

ALL PURPOSE — A blend of oils suitable for consecrating implements, dressing candles, purifying rooms, and enticing an advantageous atmosphere to any room in which it is used.

ALLSPICE — Rubbed on the feet and navel, this is said to add strength to one's will and determination, thereby assisting in gaining all objectives. It gives incentive and energy to the lazy when applied around the neckline, and can spark all who use it with the ambition to succeed in work, school, or business.

ALMOND — Said to attract money when it is added to incense. Use about one drop per spoonful of Fast Luck or Wealthy Way Incense.

      The ancient Egyptians regarded this fragrance as a symbol of wakefulness, and many moderns dab it over the eyebrows each morning upon getting out of bed to assure alertness.

ALTAR — Anoint the altar with this at least once a week, and preferably on Sunday. Place some oil in an open dish in any room to lift the vibrations to a greater, purer height so that Holy Spirits will find the room a fitting place for abode.

AMBER — Very popular in many European countries as a protection against witches, warlocks, and ill luck.

      For those who carry a Breastplate of Moses seal for protection from all harm, anoint it with this oil every seven days to intensify and prolong its effectiveness.

AMBERGRIS — This can be used in conjunction with any other oil of your choice — as well as alone for those who may select it as an enchanting personal fragrance.

      When applied along with another scent it adds strength and power to the intended purpose of the charm.

ANCIENT WISDOM — Proverbs 8, Verse II says, "For wisdom is better than rubies; and all the things that may be desired are not to be compared to it."

ANGEL — Angels, spirits, demons, and goblins may be attracted to the earthly planet when oils they like are used. This odor is pleasing to angels and should be placed near where the invocation is made, saying "Here is thy favorite oil which I have placed before thee to please thee so that thou may see my intentions are sincere and my words are truthful."

A peaceful oil, pink candles may be dressed with this to attract friends, and white candles anointed with it to calm a troubled home.

ANGER — This is used either on oneself, or others, when tempers flare and passions explode to quiet, soothe, and calm. Rub behind the ears and across the forehead for quick results, at the same time composing the mind by repeating slowly from Psalm 36, "In Thy light shall we see light. Continue Thy loving kindness unto them that know Thee, Lend Thy righteousness to the upright in heart."

ANIMAL — This is not intended for any four-footed friends, but could turn a shy miss or timid beau into an aggressive feline or ferocious tiger. Use sparingly as it is highly concentrated.

ANISE — Used by voodooists before and during rituals.

To increase one's clairvoyant abilities, add to the bath water, and anoint the premises and the body before gazing into the crystal ball or shuffling the cards for telling fortunes.

ANOINTING — In general, all oils are anointing oils as to anoint simply means to rub over with oil or to apply oil especially for consecration.

Some dealers or manufacturers may make up a particular oil by this name, to be used in magnetizing candles, on the altar or on incense burners, and on other ritual implements.

APHRODISIA — Sexy, sexy, sexy...should be used sparingly, and only when near the person you wish to arouse.

To excite great passion in another, secure for yourself a Fifth Pentacle of Venus design (draw one as pictured in the Greater Key of Solomon book or purchase it from an occult supply house), anoint with oil, and place it in the pocket or purse of the one you wish to attract.

APPLE BLOSSOM — Rub on the body to attract peace of mind and general contentment and happiness.

Add to the bath as an aid toward complete relaxation.

AQUARIUS (January 21 to February 19) — The House of Friendship. Uranus is the ruling planet. Lucky day is Wednesday. Lucky numbers are 3 and 4. While Aquarius people are of a patient, faithful, and determined nature with great possibilities, they can use their special fragrance to give them that extra "get up and go" push which they often need to accomplish the goals of which they are inherently capable.

ARABIAN NIGHTS — An attracting oil whose fragrance causes others to find you stimulating, exciting, and appealing. Use it in the bath and on the body to draw many new friends.

ARIES (March 21 to April 20)— Mars is the ruling planet. The House of Meditation and Life. Lucky day is Tuesday. Lucky numbers are 1 and 2. Noted for their push, drive, and abilities, Aries people are aggressive and courageous leaders, capable organizers, and clear, direct thinkers. They sometimes use this special oil which enhances their natural clairvoyant abilities, and in the work they can do in healing with their hands and magnetic presence.

AS YOU PLEASE — The use of this will bring success in almost any endeavor as it is formulated to overcome the objections of others to your plans. Apply it to the fingertips, soles of the feet, and the throat just before you present your idea or plans, and others will be willing to go along with your proposal.

ASTARTE — Dedicated to the Mesopotamian goddess of love who dates back to about 2000 BC, Astarte was believed to have the power to help those who wished to have a child. If that is your desire, anoint the inner thighs with this fragrance before a love session and the results may be favorable.

ASTRAL TRAVEL — There can be dangers with travelling on the astral plane and it is not recommended. However, should one decide to persist in this adventure, anoint the body at the pulse centers — particularly the wrists and temples — and chant as the oil is applied:

> Be with me on this journey
> Keep me safe and secure.
> Ease the passage there and back
> As I venture this astral tour.

ASTROLOGICAL OILS — There are twelve zodiacal blends, each one specially blended to weave a specific aura of allure and protection for those born under that sign. Each is listed by the sign for which they were created.

If you were born between:	See:
January 21 and February 19	Aquarius
February 20 and March 20	Pisces
March 21 and April 20	Aries
April 21 and May 22	Taurus
May 23 and June 21	Gemini
June 22 and July 22	Cancer
July 23 and August 22	Leo
August 23 and September 22	Virgo
September 23 and October 22	Libra
October 23 and November 21	Scorpio
November 22 and December 22	Sagittarius
December 23 and January 20	Capricorn

Each sign is ruled by a particular planet. If you do not know which planet rules your sign, see Planetary Oils where there is a list of the ruling planet for each of the twelve signs.

ATTAR OF ROSE — A potent concoction formulated for love goals — enhancing sexual powers, deepening a romantic commitment, expanding the ability to accept friendship and intimacy, or overcoming mental barriers which may have caused an avoidance of any real emotional involvement.

ATTRACTION — Should always be worn when searching for a mate. Use as a perfume, and every seven days put a few drops in the bath water to sustain a continuous personal magnetism

   For a lucky day sprinkle a few drops in the shoes you wear.

AURA — The rays which emanate can be increased and intensified by sitting so that the head and shoulders have a completely black background. Anoint the forehead and all around the neck. As the oil is applied lightly, chant softly with each stroke:

   I wish my aura to be clear
   Let it gently, simply appear.
   Reveal the colors soft and bright
   That it may shine a crystal light.

AUTUMN LEAVES — A quieting oil which soothes ruffled feelings and calms tensions. Use it in the bath, on the body, or in the home.

   Add to the palms of hands before discussing problems to instill courage, bring clearness of thoughts, and add strength to the user's point of view.

AZALEA — A fragrance for all purposes which brightens one's thoughts and eases one's burdens. Apply it each morning and pray silently:

   Bless my work this day,
   Let kindness come with all I say.
   Should I meet someone in need,
   Help me to heal, never impede.

B

BALM GILEAD — Add three drops to one's daily bath water to beautify the skin and, at the same time, enhance the spirit. Chant softly or meditate silently upon this small rhyme:

> I am me, unlike no other,
> I wish to be as good as I can,
> I want to love, but not to smother
> Those I meet through chance or plan.

BANANA — The banana grows on a palmlike plant with very large leaves which overlap at their bases to form a 'false trunk'. As the plant matures its true stem rises from the ground and pushes through the center of the 'false trunk' to emerge and become the bearer of male and female flowers. From only the female ones come bananas. The entire plant is cut down to harvest the fruit since they bear only once.

When you wish to emerge from whatever burden or misfortune is weighing you down so that you cannot flourish, use this oil as your personal scent.

BANISHING — Should you have unwanted visitors from time to time, and your cool reception has not discouraged them, write their names on a small square of parchment paper. Anoint each corner of the paper with the oil and bury the charm on the pathway to your entrance doorway. Those whose names are scribed on the talisman will soon cease their unwelcome visits.

BAPTISM — This rite of initiation begins with a ritual cleansing of washing away past transgressions with a clean cloth (a white handkerchief is suitable) dipped into tepid water to which a spoonful of hyssop has been added.

Apply the dampened cloth to the forehead, nape of the neck, and backs of the hands. As this is done, read Verses I

1. Have mercy upon me, O God, according to thy loving-kindness: according unto the multitude of thy tender mercies blot out my transgressions.

2. Wash me thoroughly from mine iniquity, and cleanse me from my sin.

3. For I acknowledge my transgressions and my sin is ever before me.

4. Against thee, thee only, have I sinned, and done this evil in thy sight that thou mightest be justified when thou speakest, and be clear when thou judgest.

5. Behold, I was shapen in iniquity and in sin did my mother conceive me.

6. Behold, thou desirest truth in the inward parts and in the hidden part thou shalt make me to know wisdom.

7. Purge me with hyssop, and I shall be clean; wash me, and I shall be whiter than snow.

After the reading, dab the thumb into the oil and rub onto the initiate's temples, ear lobes, and throat as the pastor or leader intones at each point.

I, (name) in the name of the Father, the Son, and the Holy Ghost.

Verses 8 through 15 of the same Psalm are now read:

8. Make me to hear joy and gladness; that the bones which thou hast broken may rejoice.

9. Hide thy face from my sins, and blot out all mine iniquities.

10. Create in me a clean heart, O God; and renew a right spirit within me.

11. Cast me not away from the presence; and take not thy Holy Spirit from me.

12. Restore unto me the joy of thy salvation; and uphold me with thy free Spirit.

13. Then will I teach transgressors thy ways; and sinners shall be converted unto thee.

14. Deliver me from bloodguiltiness, O God, thou God of my salvation: and my tongue shall sing aloud of thy righteousness.

15. O Lord, open thou my lips; and my mouth shall show forth thy praise.

The service is now complete and may be ended with all present reciting the Lord's prayer.

BAT'S BLOOD — One of the black arts' oils which creates discord, tension and havoc wherever it is used. Sprinkle on enemies, but not on yourself.

Use it to anoint parchment paper on which evil pacts or wicked desires have been inscribed.

A Black voodoo doll, labeled with a foe's name, and sprinkled with this oil will almost surely cause distress. Place the doll at the enemy's doorway so that it will be discovered as he enters or leaves the house or apartment.

BAYBERRY — Brings money to the pockets and blessings to the home of those who daily anoint their wrists with this legendary scent.

Sprinkle your billfold or purse with it once every seven days and never be without money.

To draw money, write the amount you need for a specific bill or purchase on a square of parchment and place the paper beneath a green candle which you have dressed with this oil. Light the candle and burn it for fifteen minutes each day until the amount required has been received.

BEND OVER — Try a bit on door knobs so that all who enter will be inclined toward you. This method also acts as protection against hexes.

If placed on each fingertip and over each temple, it is said to give one the power to bend others to your will.

BENEFICIAL DREAM — The imagery which occurs during sleep is one of the extraordinary mysteries of life. Everybody dreams but no one knows why. Some believe that all four components of a person — physical, etheric, astral, and spiritual — contribute to one's dreams. While the remembrance of dreams fade fast, they may linger long enough for an examination of their content and significance if this oil is applied to the temples and nape of the neck just before retiring.

BENZOIN — An aroma from the East, this is a very rich oil and is one of the ingredients of the holy anointing oil used in British coronations.

Witches and sorcerers use this in purification rituals.

Add Benzoin Oil to any incense to heighten its effectiveness.

Many practitioners anoint the hands and forehead with this to purify the soul before attempting any kind of occult work.

BERGAMOT — Wear in the palm of each hand to protect one from all harm and to dispel any hex which might be attempted against them.

To attract riches, rub some on the inside of your purse, pocket, or wallet.

BETTER BUSINESS — Attract customers with money to spend into your establishment by sprinkling this across the entrance each morning just prior to opening time.

To lure browsers to a particular area of the store, rub a

few drops of oil beneath the display of the goods you wish them to notice and purchase.

BEWITCHING — Not a black magic oil, but not an entirely innocent one either. It combines some angelic qualities with some devilish ones to result in an enticing, beguiling fragrance which will bind others to you with a bond of love and affection.

BIBLE BOUQUET — Place a drop on each corner of your Bible before reading so that you may understand the meaning more clearly. Anoint the throat with it before reading Psalms and their powers should be intensified.

BIG MONEY — Rub the lining of your purse, billfold, cash register, money clip, pocket — wherever you usually keep your funds — with this on the first day of each month, and every eighth day thereafter — the ninth, seventeenth, and twenty-fifth. This small rite should assure you of always having sufficient cash to cover daily needs.

BINGO — As the name itself reveals, use to enhance one's chances of winning by anointing each corner of the your card before the first number is drawn. Between each call, chant quickly and silently this rhyme:

> One, two, three, four,
> Five spaces in a row.
> Help me win, I implore,
> Fast or slow, bring my dough.

BLACK ARTS — Use this with extreme caution as it is one of the most potent of the black magic oils.

The ones who desire to bind themselves to the Devil anoint their bodies with this before signing the pact or being initiated into the cult of devil worshippers.

It is also used for crossing one's enemies by sprinkling it in their path where they will step on it and it will cling to their shoes, causing them pain wherever they go.

To play havoc with a competitor's business, go into his store and purchase a small item, paying for it with a bill which has been sprinkled with Black Arts Oil. This allegedly causes the money in the cash box to begin to shrink until it cannot cover the expenses of the business.

To counteract the effects of this oil, burn Dragon's Blood Incense daily on any premises which you think may be affected as this is the only incense whose fumes can overcome the damage which may be done by the Black Arts oil.

BLACK CAT (Also known as Cat Bone)—One of the luckiest of all scents, it is favored by gamblers. Anoint the racing form or lottery ticket on each corner.

Sprinkle it at all entrances — doors and windows — to the home so that negative entities will be unable to enter and take possession of the premises.

It can also be used as one's daily perfume. This assures that only favorable circumstances and friendly encounters will be experienced as the day progresses.

BLACK DEVIL — Said to make impotent one who is unfaithful. Just sprinkle a few drops on the clothes of the unfaithful one while they are asleep. This can be used safely as it will not affect one who has not strayed.

BLACK PANTHER — A strong, powerful blend which bestows confidence in one's own abilities to those who use it as a daily perfume. It is a favorite of salesmen who need to be aggressive in their approach to customers.

BLESSED MARY — Quick assistance will come to those who are in dire straits by use of this fragrance dedicated to the Mother of God.

Apply oil to the temples and inner wrists. Kneel and pray with sincerity for aid with your particular situation or problem:

Blessed Mary, Mother of God,
In my hour of need I call upon you.
Enfold Thy humble child into your love
Strengthen me so that I may conquer
this harmful and burdensome condition.

BLESSING OIL — If used on the body, it is believed to purify the soul.

The most popular use is to anoint altars, candles, implements, incense burners, or any ritual tools.

BLUE SONATA — A romantic scent suitable for personal use. It encourages admirers as it creates that special enticing aura. Apply the oil to a small cotton ball and place it in one's lingerie drawer.

BOSS FIX — Rub on the boss's or supervisor's chair, or sprinkle across the doorway of his office so that he is sure to walk over it. This is believed to cause the employer to look favorably upon one's work, often leading to a raise in salary and possibly a promotion to a better or more responsible position.

BOTTOM NO. 20 — Allegedly a powerful hexing mixture. Apply it on a foe's doorknob so that he will be sure to touch it. Use a cotton swab or dropper as you should not get it on your own hands as in some cases it has been said that it brings instant bedevilment and disorientation.

If you should spill any on your own self, cleanse it away thoroughly with Rosemary Oil quickly, and wait a full day before going ahead with hexing the enemy.

BOUQUET X135 — Includes most of the same ingredients as many of the lucky oils. This one brings good fortune to all areas of one's life when sprinkled in the shoes once a week.

BREAK UP — When it becomes necessary to end a relationship, this ritual can make the parting calmer and easier to bear.

Set side by side — close together — two red candles. Beneath each, place a square of parchment on which has been written the names of those who are to be separated. Light both candles and let them burn for about ten minutes. Snuff the flames, move the candles apart so there is about two inches between them. Repeat the ritual daily, moving the candles further and further apart until the purpose is accomplished.

BREAKING UP — The suffering usually accompanying partings can be eased by an application of a few drops of this onto a possession of the one who is leaving.

A piece of cloth which has been worn but not yet washed is one of the most suitable talismans. If such is not available, a piece of jewelry, a dish, book, or any item that has been touched or used by the departing party is appropriate. Sprinkle the chosen item with the oil, place it in a box or container, and seal the package securely. Place the charm in a secret place where no one else will handle it. Take it out every third day and reanoint it, but do not unseal it. This ritual will often hold the person, preventing their planned departure.

BRIDAL BOUQUET — A lady who is seeking a commitment from her loved one can hasten his decision by using as her perfume this fragrance of brides.

The lady who wears this scent on her wedding day will surely have a long and happy married life.

BRUNO'S CURSE — Rub on the bottom of feet and on the wrists as a protection from evil.

To insure yourself from sudden or violent death, secure a seal called Breastplate of Aaron and anoint it weekly with this oil.

BUDDHA — Believed to bring one into contact with the spiritual guidance of Buddha, and to stimulate latent mystical powers, when rubbed on the forehead.

      The blessings of Buddha will be conferred upon those who keep a statue of Buddha in their home and anoint it weekly with this oil.

BULL'S — To increase one's strength to massive proportions, massage this into the chest, thighs, and forearms after the bath.

      For overcoming, conquering, and controlling one's enemies, carry a Seal of Mephistophilas which has been dressed weekly at each corner with this magnetic oil.

BUSINESS — Increase traffic into the store by anointing the doorknobs and across the threshold at the entrance to the establishment. Do this daily, just before opening time.

C

CALIPH'S BELOVED — Worn as a perfume by the daring to incite sexual feelings and to attract attention. Use it in the bath for an all over lovely sensation.

CAMPHOR — A few drops added to the burner brings quick power to controlling incenses, causing all those within its sphere to favor the plans of the first person to inhale the fumes.

CANCER (June 22 to July 22) — The House of Travel and Harmony. Moon is the ruling planet. Lucky day is Monday. Lucky numbers are 8 and 9. Cancers are great lovers of home and family. They are cautious and farsighted, but with a restless disposition and somewhat changeable. This special blend will help one through the many ups and downs of life, changes of jobs, and the inevitable upheavals in circumstances, so that the pursuit of your own happiness can proceed in a serene manner.

CANDLE — A sacred oil, used for dressing and blessing candles. It can increase the power of all candles, whatever their purpose, so many use this oil first and then apply the specific oil they need for the special purpose they have in mind.

CAN'T STAY AWAY — Should a little extra help be needed to attract more friends and lovers, sprinkle the oil across the doorstep, and use it on the wrists after the daily bath.

CAPRICORN (December 23 to January 20) — The House of Business Profession. Saturn is the ruling planet. Lucky day is Saturday. Lucky numbers are 6 and 9. For these practical, ambitious, proud people, their special perfume will help them get through their disappointments and to release those inhibitions which sometimes can cause one to withdraw from the social life which we all need for a well-rounded personality.

CARNATION — Use it to anoint the head of a sick person to hasten their recovery.

Stimulates the energy, when used on one's own body.

In various rituals, it is favored for anointing incense burners.

The symbol of motherly love, this heady fragrance has potent power when one wishes to improve any relationship which is faltering. Use sparingly on the wrists, ankles, and back of the neck. Daily use, along with a cheerful attitude on your part, will cause others to treat you with affection and consideration.

CAST OFF EVIL — Be not overcome of evil, but overcome evil with good, says the Bible (Romans 12:21). A help in doing this is to pray sincerely as you anoint the temples with the oil.

Oh, Father, take this burden from my life,
Let me be free to serve Thee.
Take from me the pain of sin and vice,
Leave only love and kindness is my plea.

CAT BONE — To build the potency of your black cat bone, try soaking it overnight in this once a week. Each time this is done, the charm seems to increase its powers to attract those favorable vibrations which draw good fortune to its owner.

CEDAR OF LEBANON — Described in the Bible as a tree "of a high stature" and " the cedar of God," the symbolism includes pride, power, greatness, beauty, excellence, and prosperity — because of its luxuriant growth and length of life — as well as a symbol of the Messiah and His kingdom.

Use it daily as a perfume to instill confidence in all one's dealings. Apply it to the lips before praying so that the words will be wafted gently toward heaven and be received favorably by God. Anoint your Seal of Long Life with it to add to its powers for protecting one from misfortune and misery and insuring a lengthy stay on this earth.

CHANGO MACHO (Gold and Silver) — An exhilarating fragrance specially formulated to draw wealth. Carry with you a Seal of the Sun from the Sixth & Seventh Books of Moses. This is also called the Seal of Honor and Wealth and reputedly attracts plentiful gold, silver, and other of life's many blessings. Anoint the edges of the seal every Sunday and Thursday as these are the most auspicious days for financial enhancement.

CHERRY — Learn this rhyme, and sprinkle the oil at your entrance way.

In rainy weather, it will cheer things up,
In cold winter, it can warm the heart.
On cloudy days, it will bring the sunshine,
On lonely days, serenity it does impart.

CHERRY BLOSSOM — Wear as a perfume, or add to the bath, to cause one to become cheerful, gay, light hearted, and good humored.

CHINESE LUCK — According to legend, those who use this scent will be rewarded with the five great blessings — happiness, health, virtue, peace, and long life.

CHOCOLATE — An enticing oil which is designed to soften the hearts of all one's foes or opponents.

To have one's letter received favorably, apply a dab to the top left corner of the paper before one begins to write, and to the lower right corner when one's writing is finished.

CHYPRE — From the rockrose plant of Cyprus (the birthplace of Aphrodite), this scent was brought into England by the 12th Century Crusaders.

It is a favorite of gamblers who use it for luck when playing, and is highly regarded by business people who have contact with the public in their work. Rub some on the hands to bring great financial gains.

CINNAMON — Add to scrub waters for extra strength to bring good luck to the premises.

Used in incense to magnify its powers. Especially effective if added to Fast Luck Incense when you need extra-fast action.

Mix with Sandalwood Powder to induce powerful and intense vibrations which aid in one's meditations.

CITRONELLA — Attracts friends to the home and customers to a place of business when this pungent scent is added to the floor wash water.

Use it to anoint a Third Pentacle of Mercury design so that you will be more eloquent in letters, papers, or any writings. Keep the talisman in your stationary box and anoint it around the outer circle each time you begin writing.

CIVIT — A musk-like fragrance which has many uses: rub on the hands for protection, anoint the feet for spiritual enlightenment, and apply to the throat and beneath the breasts as a love perfume.

CLEO MAY — Creates an alluring physical appeal which allegedly will compel a man to fall deeply in love with the wearer. Also favored as a lucky oil by those who gamble.

   To gain financially in a business deal, wrap a John the Conqueror Root inside a dollar bill which you have anointed with Cleo May Oil. Place the root and bill in a red flannel bag which you carry in your pocket and touch from time to time as you discuss the business transaction with whomever else is involved. This method should assure you a good profit on the matter at hand.

CLEOPATRA — This is an exciting scent for lovers only. Rub it on the ear lobe, between fingers, and behind knees. Also place five drops upon each corner of the bed to excite the senses.

   If a lover seems to be drifting away, a potent love charm can be made by dressing seven pink candles with this oil. Write the loved one's name on seven squares of parchment, placing one beneath each candle. Light and burn one candle each evening, and before the week is up, the lover should have returned with renewed vigor and vitality.

CLOVER — A love oil which, when a drop is placed on one's pillow each evening before retiring, assures the faithfulness of one's mate.

CLOVES — Acts as an aphrodisiac when used at the base of the neck and on the thighs, allowing the user to seduce anyone he or she may choose.

COCONUT — Does "hard as a rock on the outside, sweet as honey on the inside" sound like the way you sometimes present yourself to others? Wouldn't it be better to reverse your persona and reveal some of your softness and humanity to others, holding to yourself the firmness of purpose and the consistency of your values until you need to use these qualities to gain special private objectives?

Try to match the inside with the outside to attain a balance which will bring rewards beyond your wildest expectations. Use the oil after the morning bath, applying it to the inside of the wrists and back of the ankles.

COME TO ME — Use on the bosom to attract sexual love. Very potent, so use sparingly.

To bind a lover to you, secure a red flannel bag into which you place a magnetic horseshoe, a magnetic lodestone, and a photograph of the loved one on the back of which you write both your name and that of the loved one. Draw three complete circles around the written names. Anoint the bag once a week with this oil and keep the bag beneath the mattress on which you sleep. For so long as you keep the bag and apply the oil regularly, the lover will not be either willing or able to leave you.

COMFORT — A general purpose oil to ease tensions in almost all situations. Should the mind be burdened, apply to the forehead and chant quietly several times to ease the stress.

My mind is cleared,
My pains are eased.
My spirit is made whole,
My heart is pleased.

COMMANDING — To get another to do your bidding, rub some on the palms and touch the person to be commanded, looking intently into their eyes and concentrating upon your desires.

Use it in your bath water to surround your entire body

with this royal aura.

To cause others to tremble before the words you speak, secure a Seventh Pentacle of Saturn design, anoint it with this oil around the outer edges, and hold it in the right hand when you speak.

COMPELLING — To gather great and mighty power onto oneself, anoint the body and read Psalms 12, 14, and 32. Fortified by this ritual, you will be able to coerce others to do your bidding.

To induce someone to pay you money that is owed to you, write the name of the debtor and the amount of money due on a piece of parchment. Place it beneath a purple candle which you have dressed with Compelling Oil. Burn for fifteen minutes daily until the debt is repaid.

CONCENTRATION — To free oneself of earthly fetters, many anoint themselves and form a trinity by rubbing this on the forehead, feet, and then palms of the hands. Remain in complete darkness and silence for at least fifteen minutes thereafter. Then arise to renewed energy and vitality along with the calmness of mind which enables you to cope with the problem or situation at hand.

To make the right decision on any matter, first take a warm bath to which you have added five drops of Concentration Oil. Then, dry yourself, but do not dress. Lie down nude on a firm bed or pad which you have covered with a clean white sheet. Apply the oil over the fingertips of both hands, and massage it into the forehead. Then lie still, face up, concentrating on your dilemma to the exclusion of all other thoughts. The choices should become clear, and before an hour has passed, the way you want to go will be firmly established in your mind's eye.

CONFUSION — Use to confuse enemies by sprinkling a few drops in their path. Be careful that you do not walk over the oil so that it gets on your own shoes or feet.

To get rid of a person who is making trouble for you, secure a black voodoo doll and label it with your enemy's name. If you can add to the doll some nail clippings, a snip of hair, or a scrap of the foe's clothing; this brings more power to the spell. Place the doll in a small box or paper bag, and sprinkle it with the oil. Melt some black wax (buy white wax and add a black crayon to color it) or use a black candle. Just put the wax or candle in a small saucepan over very low heat on the stove. When it is liquid, pour the black wax over the doll. Add more Confusion Oil, and bury the doll in the ground away from your home. Sprinkle the grave once a week with the oil, and your enemy will not be able to bother you for he will be too busy with his own troubles.

CONGO — All the way from its origins in central Africa, this mysterious fragrance seems to have the power to change situations and circumstances when there appears to be no reasonable hope for any improvement.

Anoint the finger tips on both hands, press them together, and chant until calmness and serenity prevails.

It matters not from where or when,
A turning doth come about.
Just bring it round without delay
And victory is mine, I have no doubt.

CONJURE — Spirits find this fragrance very appealing so sprinkle it all around the base of all candles before lighting them to attract those spirits necessary to accomplish the intention one seeks.

Use it to increase the intensity of a Fifth Pentacle of the Sun design which invokes the spirits who can transport one from any place to any other place magically, and in short time. Anoint each of the four corners of the center square on the talisman.

CONQUERING GLORY — To gain power over others, write their names on parchment and place the paper beneath a purple candle. Light the candle and repeat this little chant seven times quickly:

> (name), (name), do as I say,
> For I know what's best for you.
> (name), (name), this I pray,
> Follow me to Timbuktu.

CONTROLLING — When used on temples, brings peace of mind to the unsettled one.

To control a wayward lover, rub it on his or her body while sleeping.

To insure power over another, put three drops of oil in each of their shoes, and on the same day anoint a pink candle with the oil and burn for one-half hour. Repeat each day until the candle is consumed and your dominance is well-established.

COUNTERACTING — Rid the home of all ambivalent forces by anointing the doorknobs all through the house with this powerful fragrance. As the oil is applied, repeat this chant:

> Peace go with thee, evil spirits,
> I wish you no harm as you depart.
> Leave gently with my blessing,
> Let the healing forces start.

COURAGE — The use of this on the wrists and throat is believed to replace fear with fortitude, timidity with boldness, dread with daring, and apprehension with determination. Truly a shy person's best friend!

Add seven drops to the bath before going to apply for a job, take a test or examination, or when facing the boss to ask for a raise. It will lift the spirits so that the task can be faced with boldness and fearlessness.

Good will always overcome evil, so when you feel threatened, sprinkle this oil around your home. Use it in your bath, and pray fervently, "Yea, though I walk through the shadow of death, I will fear no evil for Thou art with me." Be amazed at the quick results obtained by those who trust the Lord.

COURT — Believers in the magical powers of fragrances always take this scent to the courtroom. Rub on the bottom of the feet and palms of the hands before entering the building in which the trial or appearance is to take place and its aroma should carry you through the proceedings with serenity and back into the free world when the legalities are concluded.

COURT CASE — Ease your way through the justice system by wearing this as your perfume whenever you are consulting with attorneys or going into court before the judge or jury. Favorable influences will be set up so that your complaint or defense will be listened to without prejudice, bias, or unfair prejudgment.

CRAB APPLE — Takes away rowdiness and unruliness when rubbed on anyone acting rambunctious or ugly. Try it on willful children, and on one whose temper flares under the influence of strong drink.

CROSSING — Used on dolls or images for hexing, or sprinkle in an adversary's path.

To bring aches and pain to a foe's hand or arm, borrow his (or her) ring and dip it in a thimble full of Crossing Oil. Wipe off with a clean square of cheesecloth and return it to its owner. As he wears it, within five days his fingers, hand, and arm should cause him anguish.

Dab a bit on an enemy's socks, or sprinkle in his shoes, to cause foot and leg trouble.

CROWN OF SUCCESS — A brand name used by a manufacturer. See Success Oil for uses.

CRUCIBLE OF COURAGE — The strength of this oil is credited with multiple attributes which enable one to face disaster with serenity, overcome misfortune and gain boldness when confronted with overwhelming odds.

Anoint the temples and pray sincerely this 3rd century prayer of Euphemia of Chalcedon. It is titled, "Strengthen Me In This Hour:"

Blessed art Thou, O Lord our God, who dwellest in the highest,

Thou whom the angels and all the powers of heaven praise and exalt unceasingly.

Thy weak and lowly handmaid calls upon Thee, who regardest the humble; strengthen me this hour with the power of Thy Holy Spirit, and show the wicked enemy of Christ that Thou art the God who didst send Thine angel to the three youths and didst drive the flame of fire out of the furnace.

Hear my prayer, O Lord, send me Thine aid.

Be not mindful of my sins and unworthiness; but, remembering Thy mercy and Thy readiness in helping them that call upon Thee, save me in this hour of my distress for the sake of Jesus Christ, Thy only Son, Our Lord.

CUMIN SEED — Attracts peace and tranquility to the home. Sprinkle across all doorways each Sunday morning before noon.

CYCLAMEN — Once used as a love potion, it is valued because of its medicinal properties, and is considered a magical charm which eases childbirth.

CYPRESS — Used as a symbol of mourning for the dead, it can bring great blessings of a spiritual nature to the living.

Brings calm and tranquility in many stubborn cases, particularly when used by parents on wayward children. Smooth onto the forearms and base of the throat.

DAMBALLAH — The powerful voodoo Serpent God was the inspiration for this potent concoction which is used to gain strength, power, and courage. Anoint the soles of the feet, palms, and throat.

DAMNATION — A crossing oil which is believed to cause great distress if rubbed on another person. Be sure of your intentions before using this potent mixture. Best results are obtained when it is applied to the foe in the evening so there is little chance it will be bathed away for several hours.

A truly havoc-wrecking spell may be made by burning an "enemy light." First, get wax (or use an already-made candle and work with it) and melt it in a small saucepan over a low fire. Color the wax black with candle coloring or a child's black crayon. If using an already-made candle, buy a black one and save this step in the proceedings. As your wax or black candle melts, add a teaspoonful of valerian herb, nine drops of Damnation Oil, and mix all together well. Remove the liquid from the stove and pour into a mold. If you do not have a regular candle mold, a good substitute is an empty milk carton. After the candle hardens, just tear away the paper carton and your candle is ready. Write your enemy's name on the candle — scratch it on with a small knife or a pen — as many times as possible so that the name is etched all over the candle's surface. Light the candle and burn it until it is completely consumed.

DARE TO WIN — Many times we defeat ourselves by not having confidence enough in our own innate talents and abilities. Use of this as one's daily perfume can impart to the wearer that extra poise and assurance needed at time of crisis to persevere and forge ahead to emerge victorious.

DESIRE ME — Inspires romance and should only be worn when one seriously wishes to attract the one he or she is dating. Apply to the shoulders, elbows, and back of the knees to entice those of the opposite sex.

DEVIL TRAP — Rub on the outside doorknobs and windowsills of the home so evil will not be able to enter the premises. Be assured of a blessed home by doing this once a week faithfully.

For personal protection from Black Magic, get a Great Pentagram Seal and keep it dressed with this oil.

DEVIL'S — A hexing oil. Rub or throw on an enemy to create strife and to cause bodily harm. Use with great caution as it can bring on tremendous damage.

Place the enemy's name on parchment and place it beneath a black candle. Anoint the candle with the oil. Before the candle is completely burned, your foe should be suffering pangs of remorse for their wrong doing.

DEVIL'S MASTER — Use to anoint candles burned to gain control over the evil intentions of others. Chant this affirmation as you light the flame.

>Victory is mine for I have
>God's eye for discerning,
>God's might to direct me,
>God's power to protect me.
>Victory is truly mine.

DEVIL'S SHOESTRING — Use it as a perfume so that you will always keep the upper hand in dealings with the opposite sex.

If you carry a charm bag of any kind, dress it weekly with this to perpetuate its powers.

DIVINE SAVIOR — Anoint the wrists and forehead with this consecrated oil formulated to attract those specific holy spirits who can assist with your petition.

Write your supplication on parchment paper and anoint each corner with a drop of the oil. Roll the paper into a cylinder shape (with the request on the inner side) and tie it securely with a white ribbon.

Select a secret place to hold the talisman and, as you deposit it there, concentrate on this prayer by an unknown author:

> God, make me brave for life;
> Oh, braver than this.
> Let me straighten after pain,
> As a tree straightens after the rain,
> Shining and lovely again.
> God, make me brave for life;
> Much braver than this.
> As the blown grass lifts, let me rise
> From sorrow with quiet eyes,
> Knowing Thy way is wise.
> God, make me brave,
> Life brings such blinding things.
> Help me to keep my sight;
> Help me to see aright,
> That out of dark comes light.

DIXIE LOVE — Charming ladies become enchantresses, and unassuming ones turn into fascinating women through the use of this attractive fragrance. It inspires flirtations, affection, and happy love affairs.

DO AS I SAY — For self-control, self-mastery, and self-confidence, one should wear this daily. It imparts such assuredness that others bend to the will of the wearer without even being aware they are under another's spell.

To get someone else to act as you wish them to, sprinkle the oil on their clothing secretly and repeat this chant nine times quickly.

> Powers of love, powers of light,

Cause this one to obey.
Powers of hate, powers of night,
Let him (her) do as I say.

DOMINATION — Used by the shy to develop will power, determination, and confidence.

To force another to your will, secure for yourself two Seals of Fire, a design from the Sixth and Seventh Books of Moses. On the back of one of the seals, write your name, and on the back of the other, write the name of the person you wish to give in to your wishes. To the other person's seal apply Controlling Powder liberally and place the seal in a small box or envelope with the design downward, the name upwards. Place your seal on top of the other, your name downward, the design upward. Sprinkle the seal with Domination Oil and close the box or seal the envelope so the seals cannot move away from one another, for as long as your Seal of Fire is moist with this oil and above the other Seal of Fire, your will in all matters should prevail.

DOUBLE ACTION — Use with the Double Action Candle to turn away malevolent forces and attract instead beneficial vibrations. Do remember that when anointing these candles, always apply the oil from the center upwards, and from the center downwards.

DOUBLE CROSS — It is held that the wearer of this will be empowered to confuse their enemies. Rub inside the elbows and back of the knees when making a deal with a difficult customer or when you are speaking to someone you wish to believe you and your words are not exactly as true as they might be.

To break up a love affair, get two black crucifix candles and dress them with this oil. Write the names of the two people you wish to divide on two pieces of parchment and place one beneath each candle. The candles should be placed side by side, touching each other, and then lighted. Burn for ten minutes and extinguish the flame. On the second day, move the two candles apart about two inches, and light them for ten minutes. On the third day, move the candles a bit further apart and light them. Repeat this for as many days as the candles last, separating them a few more inches each day.

DOUBLE FAST LUCK — An extra-strength formula for attracting fortunate and favorable circumstances which can bring a shower of blessings to every area of your life.

Apply to the soles of the shoes each morning, and your steps will guide you toward productive and advantageous opportunities in both your business and personal life.

DOUBLE HEX — This is to be used after the Hex Breaking Oil has broken the spell which was put against a victim.

Once the jinx has been nullified, it can be returned to the one who placed it by following up quickly with this retribution helper.

Write the name of the person who placed the spell with a dip pen and Black Magic Black Ink across the base of a pyramid-shaped piece of parchment. Fold the paper upward from the bottom to the center. Then bring the upper tip downward to meet the folded bottom at the center. Use sealing wax across the line where the upper and lower folded portions meet so that they will remain in place. Anoint all edges of the now hat-shaped charm with the oil and the enemy will be humbled and contrite as long as the seal is in place.

DOVE'S BLOOD — Rub on the feet when going to court, or on any peace mission.

Use on any parchment seal once a week to intensify its powers.

DRAGON'S BLOOD — An uncrossing oil used by those working on difficult cases. It is specially formulated to aid those stubborn, long-lasting conditions which have been hanging on for a long period of time.

Add some to the scrub water to rid the premises of any evil forces which may be lurking about.

To keep one's home free of wicked spirits and malevolent influences, dress a Double Action Candle liberally with the Dragon's Blood Oil and burn it completely. This candle, with the top half red in color, and the bottom half black, is symbolic of the life forces of good and evil and is designed to draw in the beneficial spirits and to turn back a curse toward its sender.

DRAW ACROSS — Cut the obstacles between an alienated friend, an estranged family member, or a straying lover with an application of this onto a note to the one you wish to draw closer.

Write the message honestly — acknowledging any portion of the estrangement which may be your responsibility, and offering to negotiate a common ground of agreement.

Follow this procedure: anointing the envelope also with the oil and it will almost surely follow that a reconciliation is effected before the next full moon wanes.

DRAW BACK — Scratch the names of the person you desire to return to your life into the red portion only of a Double Action Candle, and anoint that half with the oil as you chant nine times:

Come back, come back to me,
Return in peace is my plea.
Come back, come back to me,
Your face I ache to see.

DRAWING — A powerful force for bringing money, luck, or love to the one who wears this as a perfume.

To lead one to the place where money will be found, place a Southern John the Conqueror Root in a red flannel bag and anoint the bag with this oil. Many believe that the person who carries this bag, and dresses it with the Drawing Oil every third day, will never be broke.

To draw à wandering lover home, mix this oil with some plain salt in a small dish. Hold a small portion of this in the palm of the hand and blow it in each direction — north, east, south, and west. Wherever the lost one is, they will be drawn back to the place where this spell is performed. Do it daily until the lover's return.

DREAM — A few drops on the pillow is often helpful in inducing quiet restful sleep accompanied by good influences, and sometimes prophetic dreams or visions.

DRESSING — An all-purpose anointing oil for consecrating candles, homes, altars, amulets, seals, etc.

DRIVE AWAY EVIL — Hurtful and harmful vibrations will be swept away by the seductive fragrance when this is applied to the outside doorknobs of all entrances to the premises.

E

EARTH — To protect your bit of this planet, sprinkle a drop at each corner of your property, home, apartment, car, and anoint all particular items of special value. Each morning, upon awakening, recite this simple blessing.

Mother Earth, upon which I dwell,
This day I do wish thee well.

For confidence in yourself and your own small private portion of the universe, use this confidence building scent to bolster personal serenity and optimism. Use the oil as your perfume and take to heart these few lines from Shakespeare's Timon of Athens.

Long have I loved what I behold.
The night that calms,

the day that cheers;
The common growth of mother-earth
Suffices me.

EASY LIFE — Apply with gentle strokes on the shoulders, neckline, and arms to attract the good life with health, blessings, abundance, great fortune, happiness, and a comfortable old age.

To keep every month filled with fortunate happenings, on the first day of the month dress a green candle with the oil and burn for ten minutes. Do this each day for five consecutive days. On the sixth day, put five drops of oil on a sheet of parchment paper which is then lit and burned to ashes. Place the ashes in a red flannel bag and carry them on your person for the remainder of the month, anointing the bag every fifth day with five drops of the Easy Life Oil.

EASY TIMES — For this ritual which is dedicated to improving your personal and financial conditions, use any plain band ring. An old one of no value or a new inexpensive one is recommended as you will not be wearing it again.

Place the ring in the center of a clean white handkerchief. Then make four folds in the cloth. The first fold is made from the top edge downward to just below the center. Then fold the bottom edge up to the top. Next fold the left edge to the right edge, and finally from right to left. Thus the ring is protected.

Tie the talisman securely with green ribbon or thread so that it cannot be opened or the ring lost accidentally, chanting as you bind the charm:

>Easy come, and easy go,
>May the good times flow.
>Bring me money, love, and luck,
>Many friends, and lots of pluck.
>Carry the talisman in your purse or pocket at all times.

EGYPTIAN GLORY — Dedicated to Thoth, the lord of wisdom and magic, this can help you attain your own goals in these areas.

When faced with a difficult decision, anoint the temples with the oil and pray with sincerity and confidence:

> Lord of all knowledge and understanding,
> impart unto this humble on the insight
> and the strength needed so that I may emerge
> from this quandry with the wisdom and assurance
> that blesses and strengthens those in need.

ENCHANTMENT — The use of this as a perfume builds a spellbinding attractiveness for its user.

Try three drops in the morning bath for all day long-lasting allure.

ENEMY — This oil is mixed with both protective and repulsing elements. It should be rubbed completely around the neck, starting at the middle of the throat in front and going all the way around to the middle of the back at the top of the spine. Then again from the middle of the throat in front around to the back of the neck, completing and closing the circle. Use this any time you are in contact with an enemy or one you do not trust, thereby destroying any influence they may have on you.

ENVY — Should the destructive pangs of envy hold you from living the serene carefree life to which one is entitled, remove these destructive chains by anointing the forehead, ear lobes, and throat. As each area is touched, chant with conviction:

> I am not jealous, I do not envy thee.
> I am content with my personal situation.
> No other can take from me this serenity
> For I am secure and happy with me.

EUCALYPTUS — Believed to be a strong healing oil. Use on finger tips, inside of wrists and the temples.

For one who is hurt, depressed, or ill, this oil applied to

the affected area will help until the sick one can get to a doctor. As the oil is rubbed on the body in a circular motion, repeat this chant:

> Illness, sickness, fade away,
> I seek a higher healing ray,
> Bring relief from this pain,
> Make my spirit whole again.

EVE — Stimulates men. Can be used by ladies as a perfume, or by men as a nature builder.

EVIL EYE — A bit on each temple is said to avert the Evil Eye and protect from being afflicted with this condition.

To throw the Evil Eye on others, wear some above each brow.

For complete protection, carry in your pocket a handmade talisman enclosed in a red flannel bag and anoint it weekly with the Evil Eye Oil. To make your personal talisman, draw the Sacred Eye on a piece of parchment, and surround the Eye with your name by signing it all around the edge, writing your name over and over as many times as necessary to encircle the edges of the paper.

EXODUS — Sprinkle on the clothing of one you wish to depart from your area.

Use a voodoo doll (any color will do) to represent the one you wish to remove themselves from your life. Pin or tie on the name tag, and on the back of the tag write "move" nine times. Saturate the feet of the doll with Exodus Oil. Wrap the doll in a green cloth and put it away in a safe place. Every third day take the doll out and moisten the feet again until your purpose has been accomplished.

EXORCISM — To expel any alien or evil spirits which may reside within the mind or body, anoint the wrists, ankles, and forehead daily, repeating each time, "Bless me, and cast all evil from my body, all wickedness from my mind, and all sin from my soul." Repeat Psalm 62 after each anointing. This ritual will soon leave you free of all malevolent forces.

F

FANTASY — Concocted by one who believes that the particular combination of fragrances used in this mixture will cause dreams to come true — will make one fortunate in all one's endeavors so that you will have financial security, your dream home, an abundant sex life, and have the peace and security of a full, rewarding life.

FAST LUCK — Said to bring material wealth into the environment of the wearer.

Favored by those who play games of chance, but used by all who need sales, business, or profits in a hurry.

For mighty spirit forces to come to your aid when your luck seems to be fleeing, lay a buckeye between two candles — a green to the left and a white to the right. Anoint the buckeye and both candles with oil. Light the candles and let them burn completely. Then place the buckeye in a red flannel bag along with a Seal of Magic which is designed to bring magical assistance to one's wishes, desires, needs, or requests. Carry the bag with you at all times, anointing it every seventh day with the Fast Luck Oil.

FAST MONEY — Anoint each bill you get as it arrives in your possession. Place a drop of oil at each of the paper's corners, and chant as you do this.

> Bring the cash to fill this need,
> I pray it will come right away.
> Bring the money here this day,
> For (amount of debt) I now plead.

FIERY COMMAND — A powerful fragrance which is immensely popular with those impatient ones who not only want their desires met, but want them met NOW!

Obviously your requirements must be conveyed to the one you wish to fulfill them. This can be accomplished in personal conversation directly, or by written communication.

If the request is made in person, arrange to apply to the other party a dab of the oil onto the wrist, ankle, or neckline.

Should you submit your request in a letter, anoint the corners of the paper you use with the fragrance.

After the petition has been made, anoint your own wrists, ankles, or neckline at bedtime as you repeat three times this affirmation:

> East, west, north and south,
> I am surrounded with fulfillment.
> South, north, west and east
> My desires will soon be realized.

Repeat the evening ritual daily until your goal has been accomplished.

FIERY WALL OF PROTECTION — While similar to the Protection Oil, and can be used for the same objectives, this is a specially effective formula for instances where one is felt unduly pressured by another person.

Hang a wooden cross or crucifix just inside the entrance you ordinarily use when entering or exiting the home. Each time you come in or go out, and whenever the door is opened to admit a visitor, simply apply to the cross a dab of the oil as you chant quickly.

> Holy Jesus, be with me
> Protect this one that you do see.
> Guard my home night and day
> And from all foes there may be.

FINANCIAL LUCK — English essayist Joseph Addison wrote these enlightening lines about being lucky:

I never knew an early-rising, hard-working,
prudent man, careful of his earnings, and
strictly honest,who complained of bad luck.
A good character, good habits, and iron industry
are impregnable to the assaults of all the
ill-luck that fools ever dreamed of.

Copy the simple quotation and tape it where you will see it every morning — the bathroom mirror is a convenient place. Read it, and anoint the ankles and wrists with the oil. Go forth with the assurance that "today will be a financial success."

FIRE OF LOVE — Strengthens affections between two lovers when applied to both foreheads.

Use before lovemaking to cause increased passions and heightened sensitivity to both man and woman.

To start a flame in someone's heart, dress a red candle with this oil. Place beneath the candle a Seal of Love with your name and the name of the one you wish to love you on the back. As you light the candle, repeat this chant three times. Let the candle burn for ten minutes and then extinguish the flame as you repeat the chant for three more times. Do this daily until the entire candle is consumed.

Burn, flame, light this love,
Bright as the stars above.
Cause this heart to beat for me,
Light this love so all can see.

FIVE CIRCLE — Mediums anoint their body with this so they will be guided through the five auras.

Those who use it in the bath believe it will keep them surrounded with circles of faith, love, friends, health, and life itself.

FIVE FINGER GRASS — An extremely protective oil which is made to protect one from any harm which the hand of man could bring.

At the same time it strengthens the five senses — sight, hearing, touch, taste, and smell.

FLAME OF DESIRE — This is to be used by one who is endeavoring to entrap a reluctant lover, for it is said to be truly virtually irresistible when one is caught unaware by its bewitching aroma.

FLAMING POWER — Increase one's authority over others, sway opinions toward your point of view, or dominate and control situations which are of value to you with this personal scent.

Apply the oil to the earlobes and inner wrists. As each dab is smoothed onto the body, repeat these lines from Alfred Tennyson's writings:

Self-reverence, self-knowledge, self-control,

These three alone lead life to sovereign power.

FLYING DEVIL — A voodoo concoction with a great reputation for fighting off the effects of any oppressing wanga which may have been posed by an enemy. It has been known to work when other methods and remedies have failed.

Use it in the scrub water to cleanse the home, or in the bath for personal purification.

FOLLOW ME — Same purposes as Follow Me Boy — for winning law suits, court cases, gaining the upper hand in arguments or disputes, and to entice others to follow your wishes and suggestions without question or argument. Use as your daily perfume.

FOLLOW ME BOY — One of the most famous of all occult oils. Always used to beat court cases, and to win arguments.

To bend another person to your will, get two candles, one purple, one white. Write your name on parchment and place it beneath the purple candle. Write the other person's name on parchment and place it beneath the white candle. Leave the white candle undressed, but anoint the purple candle with Follow Me Boy Oil. Get several (the exact number does not matter) pieces of yarn or string about seven or eight inches in length. Tie the strings around the white candle, spaced about one inch apart, from top to bottom. Light both candles and, as the white candle burns down, and the strings break, that person's defenses against you will collapse.

FORGET HER OR FORGET HIM — These oils are compounded to help one consign to oblivion painful memories of a lost love or a broken affair. Use it daily, morning and evening, on the forehead and behind the ears. You will find that the pain of loss is fading quickly and soon only the present and the future will fill your life and your mind.

FORGET ME NOT — When a lover is going away, whether for a few hours or a long period of time, wear this beguiling fragrance and the separation will be easy — knowing you will stay in the loved one's mind while you are apart.

FOUR LEAF CLOVER — The fragrance inspired by this universally accepted good luck charm is four-fold.

> As immortalized in the words of a popular song,
> One leaf is sunshine,
> The second is rain, (as needed for all living things)
> Third is for roses, that grow in the lane.
> The one remaining is for "somebody I adore".

Do not overlook adding a touch of this to the wrists and throat daily to insure a magical, marvelous, miraculous, merry day!

This popular lucky symbol is also believed by many to give its owner psychic powers. Carry your talisman in a red flannel bag, anointing it once a week, so that it may bring insight into situations which you have not previously been able to understand.

FRANGI PANI — An attraction oil which is worn as a perfume. It causes others to confide secrets, confess indiscretions, and trust the user implicitly.

To attract love, respect, and admiration carry with you a Third Pentacle of Venus design and anoint it weekly with this oil.

FRANKINCENSE — A sacred oil for anointing objects and to bring many blessings.

Also, this oil can allegedly free one from the obsession of drugs or drink, cigarettes, unhealthy relationships, over-eating, and other destructive habits. Write on parchment paper with Dove's Blood Ink the habit or condition of which you wish to rid yourself. On the other side of the paper, write your name, and place the paper in a small dish with the name facing upward. Sprinkle it daily with three drops of oil, each morning and evening, and pray that the bondage of unhealthy habits or behavior will be taken away from you by repeating prayerfully, "Be with me this day and help me to respect my body, my mind, and my soul. Instill in me the love of self and God, nourish me with Thy bountiful blessings, and assist me to overcome the temptations put before me each day.

FRANKINCENSE & MYRRH — As recorded in Matthew, Chapter 2, Verse 11, the three wise men came to the baby Jesus and, "when they had opened their treasures, they presented unto him gifts: gold, frankincense, and myrrh."

When two of these are combined into a single oil, the fragrance reputedly has great influence for healing, enhancing one's native abilities, for protecting against evil forces, or in baptisms.

FREE FROM EVIL — For security of the home, anoint the outside of entry doorknobs once a week as you pray this devotion.

Guard this abode with Thy love,
Protect it from all evil intent.

May all within reside in peace,
As love and trust doth increase.

FRENCH CREOLE — A multi-purpose oil, very popular with those who believe in its powers to make one's dreams come true.

It is an attracting agent also, being favored by many who use it to draw lovers and good fortune.

To arouse desire in another, secure from the person you wish to excite a few genital hairs and place them in a red flannel bag along with seven cloves and a whole beth root. Anoint the bag weekly with the French Creole Oil and keep it secreted among his (or her) clothes.

FRENCH LOVE — A powerful sexually attracting fragrance which is to be used daily but sparingly to draw friends and lovers.

After the bath, apply to the back of the neck, around the ankles and wrists, and behind the knees. As you go about your daily routine, be quick to smile, slow to anger, and always willing to extend friendship to all you encounter.

Each morning, read and take to heart these few lines from Henry Wadsworth Longfellow's writing:

Talk not of wasted affection,
affection never was wasted.
If it enrich not the heart of another,
its water, returning back to their springs,
like the rain,
shall fill them full of refreshment.
That which the fountain sends forth
returns again to the fountain.

FRIENDSHIP — Used by those who are shy and afraid of people. This oil should encourage just enough assertiveness on the wearer's part to make others aware of the pleasantness and sociability necessary to break the ice and encourage friendliness.

FRUIT OF LIFE — This combination of essential oils brings together those elements which are reputedly advantageous for enticing the forces of the universe which bring favors from the gods of love, good fortune, financial wealth, loyalty from friends, good health, and abundant success in one's chosen profession.

Use daily, anointing the forehead, wrists, ankles after the morning bath.

G

GALANGAL — Often made with bits of the genuine galangal root in the bottle, this is most often used when going to court, for it is believed that the judge will always rule in favor of the one whose feet and arms are anointed with this oil.

GAMBLER'S — Place a drop or two in each palm and rub vigorously before gambling.

If you play bingo, anoint each corner of your card with this before the first number is called.

For a potent gambling hand, place in a red flannel bag some Samson's Root, Devil's Shoestring, and Grains of Paradise. Feed the bag every nine days by dowsing it with this oil and things should soon begin to come your way.

GARDENIA — A protective oil which will stop others from creating strife in your life.

GEMINI (May 23 to June 21) The House of Versatility and Education. Mercury is the ruling planet. Lucky day is Wednesday. Lucky numbers are 3 and 8. Geminis are ruled by the heart instead of the head, are sensitive and idealistic. They need the assistance of a special scent which can be relied upon to calm their restless nature, to soothe the tensions which plague their lives and to help them out in any emergency.

GERANIUM — Said to act as a hex-breaker. Use anytime you feel burdened or oppressed as it lifts the spirits and disperses any ill-intentioned influences in the vicinity.

GET AWAY — Rub on door knobs and windowsills to turn back all evil spirits, unfavorable influences, or unwelcome visitors.

To be protected against all phantoms of the nights which may cause restless sleep or nightmares, obtain for yourself a Fifth Pentacle of the Moon design, anoint it with the oil every seven days, and keep the talisman beneath your pillow.

GINGER — Adds spice to all one's relationships. When life seems dull, dull, dull, just apply to the back of the knees, elbows, and behind the ears before going out of the house — a delightful day of fun and excitement is apt to follow.

GINGER BLOSSOM — Used as a cologne, this alluring fragrance is designed to stimulate one's affections and romantic inclinations.

GINSENG — The scent dedicated to the most lauded herb in history; known as Man Root, Heal-All, Root of Life, Wonder of the World, etc.

It is applied to the feet in the belief that it will direct them toward the most advantageous path.

Apply it to the palms of the hands so that one can reach out toward friends and business opportunities.

Anoint the soles of the feet that they may be directed into a righteous path, avoiding the allure of evil ways.

GLORY — To enjoy glory before men is to be known and honored on account of one's character, qualities, position, possessions, or achievements. So if you are lacking in any of these areas, wear this oil as a perfume so that you will gain the confidence you need to act as though you possessed all these attributes, and people will never know if your characteristics are real or imaginary.

GLOW OF ATTRACTION — A brand name used by some firms for their Attraction Oil. It has the same uses and attributes.

GO AWAY — This is one of the most potent of the controlling oils, and can quickly help banish an unwelcome visitor to the home. Simply dampen a small cloth or a cotton ball with the scent and secrete the amulet in or near where the caller stands or sits. Within a short while, the intruder will remember other appointments and depart.

Encourage a person you do not wish to have near your home to move on by securing one of their stockings or socks without their knowledge. Dampen the foot of the charm and tie it to the bumper of a nearby parked car. When the owner of the vehicle drives away, your unwanted visitor, tenant, or relative will become restless and soon leave the premises.

GODDESS — Specially prepared for those women who wish to be treated royally by all those with whom they come in contact, who want respect more than love, and admiration more than intimacy. Wear it when meeting strangers and make a real high-class impression.

GOLD & SILVER — Use as a daily perfume to entice fun and excitement into your home and life.

To encourage others to lend or give you money, sprinkle a drop or two into the palms of your hands and, when in the presence of the one you think can satisfy your monetary needs, place your hands on their body — shaking hands, hugging them, or in some other surreptitious manner. Soon after the gesture, make a plea for the favor you need.

Attract customers to a place of business by sprinkling it across the doorway each morning just before the doors are opened. Invite good fortune by repeating this chant as you apply each drop.

> My heart is pure, my soul is clean,
> I deserve great riches I've never seen.
> More and more money — paper, silver, gold,
> It will increase to great wealth untold.

GOOD LUCK — A Yiddish proverb says that an ounce of luck is better than a pound of gold. Whether you have need of the good fortune or the money, use this to draw both.

Each morning, after the bath or shower, enhance the entire day by using the oil on back of the knees, at elbows, and behind the ears. This assures favorable circumstances in all your dealings all day long.

Anoint the hands before playing any game of chance. Place a drop on each corner of lottery tickets. When dealing cards, apply the fragrance to the palms when cutting the deck.

GOOD TIME — All occasions, both social and business, will be enhanced by a sprinkling of this at the entrance of the place where the event is to take place. It seems to lift the spirits of all who come in contact with this distinctive fragrance.

Use it as a perfume when attending any important affair to allay any apprehensions you may be harboring about the success of the event.

A drop on the doorstep can bring good fortune to the home.

A drop behind each ear can entice pleasant, uplifting thoughts and better powers of concentration.

A drop in the shoe may guide one toward those persons who are friendly and accommodating.

A drop on each wrist encourages putting the hands to use at productive labor.

GOONA GOONA — Creates an atmosphere of trust and understanding when used in troubled situations. Apply to the body as a perfume to reduce tension when dealing with difficult people.

In the home, rub on table legs, arms of chairs, or bottoms of plates to create a calm and confident environment.

GRAPE — As well as being a tantalizing perfume for the bold and daring ones who like the unusual, this oil is gaining in popularity as a money attracting aroma. Anoint the billfold or purse with it weekly.

GRIS GRIS — This popular anointing oil has many uses, and can be used for good or evil.

Should you need to contact spirits of the other world, hold in your palm — the left if the purpose is for harm, the right if for good — the Grand Symbol of Solomon, a talisman from the Sixth & Seventh Books of Moses. Sprinkle three drops of the oil onto the paper and clutch it tightly in the clenched fist.

Concentrate on your objective for one full minute or more, and chant this plea:

>Oh Legba, make me stout of heart,
>Let my works be harkened to.
>Oh Legba, drive the evil spirit from me
>and bring success to my plea.
>Oh Legba, let my sight penetrate the innermost things,
>and give me power to speak.
>Oh Legba, never leave me.

GUARDIAN ANGEL — When in search of help with any difficulty, anoint the forehead with this sacred oil, and pray sincerely with head bowed until peace and serenity envelops your entire being.

>Holy guardian angel,

My sweet companion,
Guide me, stay with me,
Night and day,
Day and night. Amen.

Once tranquillity has been restored, one can then proceed orderly with the steps necessary to solve the problem at hand.

ŋ

H & H — Variously called Hate and Harm, Hex and Hell, Hurt and Havoc — or any combination of such titles — this is a potent blend and is to be used cautiously.

If possible, get a possession from the foe such as a key, handkerchief, sock, shoe, piece of jewelry — anything of a personal nature. Should this be impossible, use a new article which has not been worn or used by anyone else.

Place the selected item on a new piece of black material. Write the name of the enemy on a square of parchment with Dragon's Blood Ink and add this in the package.

Wrap the black cloth securely around the object and tie it with white cord or ribbon tightly into as small as possible package. Dig a hole in the ground and bury the charm. Sprinkle the oil over the top as you chant three times this verse:

Hell and highwater will come to thee,
Till your vileness has withdrawn.
Neither healthy nor hearty will they be,
Lest a metamorphosis you've undergone.

Ere the next new moon appears, the power of the foe will be so weakened that it can cause no harm at all.

HAITIAN JUNGLE — A hexing scent for use when other methods seem to have failed.

To cause an adversary to be faced with failure in any planned schemes, rub this on the foe's shoes, add to the water in which clothes are washed, or apply directly to the skin if this method is possible and feasible. Use sparingly and with discretion.

HAPPINESS — Surround yourself with the cheerfulness, pleasure, contentment, gaiety, and general feeling of well-being which is so necessary to attain happiness for yourself and those around you.

HAS NO HANNA — Anoint your purse with it, once a day, and it is claimed you will never be without money.

Worn on the body, it is reputed to keep your loved one close to you.

HEALING — Said to be vitalizing when used by convalescents.

Dispels fatigue and tiredness in all wearers.

HEALTH DRAWING — For one in ill health, the first requisite is to have a complete physical examination by a reputable physician. Follow the doctor's instructions on diet, exercise, and lifestyle precisely for a full recovery.

Should additional support be desired, anoint daily the affected area, or apply to the wrists and ankles, as one chants this healing mantra:

I am whole, I am well,
Good health and well being is my fate.
I am complete, I am well,
Good health and well being I anticipate.

HEART'S DESIRE — This may be that added bit of assistance needed to entice others to assist you in satisfying your requirements.

If a written request is being sent, anoint the stationery at each corner before the letter is sent, chanting at each point.

> Bless this message I do send,
> Grant the request I make.
> To this appeal I beg quick work,
> Bring the help fore next I wake.

HEATHER — The broomsticks on which witches of the past rode to the sabbats were traditionally made of heather.

Today the fragrance is considered a bringer of good luck, and that is what this oil can do for those who wear it as their perfume.

HEBREW — As, in the face of unsurmountable odds, the Lord parted the Red Sea so that Moses could lead the Hebrews out of danger, so this oil can protect you from your enemies and show you the way to a better life.

HELIOTROPE — The heliotrope's flowers always turn toward the sun (leading to the belief that the planets determine the time of its flowering), so direct your life toward cheerfulness, brightness, and sunshine by wearing this oil which protects from all physical harm and at the same time attracts wealth.

HELPING HAND — This is particularly suited for assistance in legal matters.

Should one have to appear in court, sprinkle a few drops on one's handkerchief. During the proceedings, hold the handkerchief in the left hand and meditate upon Verse 1, Psalm 121:

> I will lift up mine eyes unto the hills,
> From whence cometh my help.
> Be confident that the result will be one which is
>   favorable.

HEMLOCK — Secure a talisman dedicated to the black magic

spirit, Paimon, who was a great king and very obedient unto Lucifer. He can confer upon the petitioner the strength to influence and control others, subjugating them to one's demands.

On the reverse of the talisman write the favor one is in need of, and the name of the person of which the accommodation is required. This should be scribed with Dove's Blood Ink.

The seal is then wrapped in white cloth. With white thread sew all edges securely so the seal remains in place. Secrete the talisman in a dark place, removing every third day to add three drops of oil.

Once the objective is attained, burn the entire charm and bury it outside the home at the furthermost edge of ones property.

HENRY'S GRASS — Use as a personal perfume, add to any incense to increase its vibrations, or use it to anoint candles, especially the Seven Knob candles on which you have made wishes.

HEX BREAKING — Remove any curse which may have been placed upon one by sprinkling a few drops at all entrances to the home or property. As this is done, chant three times at each point:

Demon, Devil, begone from here,
Darken my abode no more.

Repeat the anointing of the premises every ninth day until all alien forces have been removed.

HEXING — Influence others to grant favors, follow your directions, and do your bidding without argument or resistance.

Anoint a black candle with the oil and, as it is lighted, repeat this affirmation:

Damn the foe who has harmed me,
May evil return to its source tenfold.
Let the sufferings intended me
be visited upon the perpetrator.

HIGH ALTAR — Use in the home, church, or other meeting places — where ever one wishes to invite the benevolent spirits to enter and be pleased with the surroundings.

Sprinkle across the entrance as you pray your own or this small petition:

Enter here, holy spirits,
Bless this sacred place.
You are welcome here
Shower it with your grace.

HIGH CONQUERING — Use before entering a battle, an argument, or court trouble. Repeat Psalm 23 and rub oil on inside of the arms from wrist to elbow. Very powerful.

HIGH JOHN — Same attributes as John the Conqueror oil, aiding the wearer in all efforts and enhancing one's mental abilities.

This brings about favorable results in all one's undertakings.

HIGH JOHN THE CONQUEROR — Same uses as High John and John the Conqueror oils.

HIGH POTENCY — This is reputedly a potent sexual stimulant and may be used as a perfume to attract friends and lovers.

For added influence, carry in purse or pocket a Seal of Merbulis (also known as the Seal of Special Attraction) which you have anointed with the oil. This intensifies the powers to captivate and control others.

HINDU GRASS — Anoint the temples to draw wisdom from the masters so that correct decisions can be made in times of stress.

In the Hindu religion, it is believed that the essence of a god descends upon earth and assumes the form of an animal, monster, or man. These gods on earth are avatars, and one of the most famous of these is The Fish who saved Manu from the Deluge by forewarning him of the danger, commanding him to build a boat, and finally towing the boat to a mountain top. The wearing of Hindu Grass oil may save you from disaster.

HOLD MY MAN — The lady who lives with doubts of her loved one's fidelity may decide to employ the magnetizing qualities attributed to this enticing fragrance.

Anoint a pink candle with the oil, from the top downward.

Beneath the candle place a Seal of Venus from the Sixth & Seventh Books of Moses on which a drop of oil has been placed at each of the four corners, and your lover's name scribed on the reverse.

Light the candle as you chant four times this rhyme:
True to me, I ask you be,
Dare not to stray away.
I beg you be true to me,
Or you will rue the day.

HOLD YOUR MAN — The purpose of this fragrance is quite similar to Hold My Man, and the ritual given above is appropriate for this oil also.

Any woman who simply uses it as her daily perfume will find that men are inclined to perk up and notice her when they come within the aura of this enchanting fragrance. It is then up to her to flirt a bit if he appears to be someone with whom she would like to become better acquainted.

HOLY — A sacred oil for blessing of altars, candles, talismans, and persons.

In the original Black and White Magic book by Marie Laveau, she suggests that the man or woman in bad luck place in a chamois bag a lodestone, a pair of Adam & Eve Roots, and a piece of Devil's Shoestring. Seal the bag and hold it in the left hand. With the right hand sprinkle five drops of Holy

Oil on it and at the same time read Psalm 23. Then carry the bag close to the body, allowing no one to touch it.

HOLY DEATH — When someone you love becomes seriously or terminally ill, nothing can take away the fear, the sadness, and the pain. First must come acceptance of the situation. Only after that can the comfort and solace which is sorely needed be attained.

Apply the oil to the wrists and ankles and take to heart John Donne's short poem which will calm and strengthen one during this tragic travail:

> Death, be not proud, though some have called thee
> Mighty and dreadful, for thou are not so:
> For those whom thou think'st thou dost over-throw
> Die not, poor Death, nor yet canst thou kill me.
> From rest and sleep, which but thy pictures be,
> Much pleasure, then from thee much more must flow;
> And soonest our best men with thee to go —
> Rest of their bones and souls' delivery!
> Though'rt slave to fate, chance, kings, and desperate men,
> And dost with poison, war, and sickness dwell;
> And poppy or charms can make us sleep as well,
> And better than thy stroke. Why swell'st thou then?
> One short sleep past, we wake eternally,
> And Death shall be no more: Death, thou shalt die.

HOLY TRINITY — Specially blended for consecrating holy implements and for anointing a crucifix before prayers. Wet the ball of the thumb with the oil, and make the sign of the cross at the bottom, the top, and tip of each arm of the crucifix, repeating this prayer, "Blessed Jesus, before Thy face I humbly pray and beseech Thee to fill my heart with feelings of faith, hope, and charity. I am truly sorry for all my sins. Strengthen my desire to turn away temptation, to have less faults today, and to resist whatever would draw me into sin."

HONEY — A new occult fragrance which is recognized as having seductive, enticing qualities. Use it as a perfume, or place a drop on one's pillow to bewitch a straying or hesitant lover.

HONEYSUCKLE — Many attributes are given this oil — rub on the money box or cash register to attract business, dab under the eyes to sharpen intuition, or anoint the palm to instill confidence when meeting those who may be important to you.

For a mighty luck charm, take a small square of genuine parchment (the skin will last longer, but paper will do) and draw on it a four-leaved clover. Your artistic abilities do not affect the power of the talisman. Use Dove's Blood Ink for the original drawing. Then each day, trace the design with this oil by using a sharpened match stem, a tooth pick, or a regular dip pen. As the design fades from the oil, the virtues of the clover — wealth, love, fame, and health — should become a part of your daily life.

HORN OF PLENTY — For great wealth and other awards and esteem, carry with you at all times a design known as the Second Pentacle of Jupiter. This is one of the many magical seals of Solomon which can be found in the Greater Key of Solomon. The design is "proper for acquiring glory, honors, dignities, riches, and all kind of good, together with great tranquility of mind; also to discover treasures and chase away the Spirits who preside over them".

Every Sunday anoint the edges of your talisman to keep its powers potent. Protect the seal by wrapping it in a clean white cotton cloth.

HOT FOOT — Long available only as a powder, it is now offered in a convenient oil, making it easier to use and not recognizable on sight by the one it is used against.

Place under the shoes, or in the path of an unwelcome neighbor who will soon become dissatisfied with their abode and will decide to make their home elsewhere.

HOTEI — The Japanese god of good luck may be attracted to this scent, and can aid those who wear it as a perfume or add a few drops to the daily bath.

When in need of immediate assistance, chant this simple petition:

Hotei, Hotei, god of good luck,
Turn to me and meet my eye.
Hotei, Hotei, god of much luck,
Help me now, not by and by.

HOUSE BLESSING — Bring untold benefits into your house or apartment with this enticing fragrance. Sprinkle it across the entrance to the home as this rhyme is chanted:

Come in my friend, come in.
Bring with you only a smile
And a heart filled with kindness.
Welcome, friend, tarry a while.

Repeat this ritual weekly, preferably on Thursday for this is the day during which one can gain money, achieve good health, establish friendships and — if so inclined — become invisible.

HUMMINGBIRD — The man who has this rubbed on his thighs and private parts by the woman who loves him will not be able to escape from her advances.

HYACINTH — Attracts love and luck when used as a perfume.

Sprinkle on the pillow for relief from insomnia as it brings peace of mind and restful sleep.

HYPNOTIC — Used by those who wish to increase their powers of concentration when practicing hypnosis. As its scent is soothing, quieting, and relaxing, the subject is more susceptible to the suggestions of the hypnotist. Place an open bottle in the room where the work is being done, or rub it around the neck of the one who is being hypnotized.

HYSSOP — A holy anointing oil. Dress all blessing candles, altars, and tools with this before using them.

It is a great additive to the bath, and a few drops of this is much less expensive than the commercial hyssop baths offered by dealers. Read Psalm 20 before bathing for many blessings to come into your life.

J

I CAN MORE THAN YOU CAN — For those involved in a competition, contest, or simply a struggle for authority over another person or an unpleasant situation, this can be utilized to gain the advantage.

Sprinkle all entrances to the home — windowsills and doorways — weekly with the oil. At the same time, wear it as your perfume. With this protection, others will be unable to beat you in either a personal or professional situation.

As you apply the oil, chant three times the words of the Roman poet, Ovid, who lived from 43 BC to 18 AD:

"Courage conquers all things; it even gives strength to the body."

I CAN, YOU CAN'T — Whenever it is felt that someone may want to diminish you in any way — trying to wrest your job for themselves, flirting with your mate or lover, spreading untrue rumors which reflect on your good character, or such — sprinkle this oil on anything the enemy will touch. The handle of a cup, steering wheel of their car, a bracelet, ring, necklace, house key, a piece of clothing, are just a few suggestions.

After the charm is set, spend no further thought or energy on the problem; it will be taken care of in its time and in a way which will be to your advantage and benefit.

IMPOSSIBLE OBJECTIVE — With a clear and definite purpose in mind, a firm determination to succeed, and devoted concentration of the goal you wish to attain, successes far beyond one's greatest hopes can be assured.

Anoint the temples with the oil as you chant this small petition from the 17th Century English essayist, Joseph Addison:

> If you wish success in life,
> make perseverance your bosom friend,
> experience your wise counsellor,
> caution your elder brother,
> and hope your guardian genius.

INDIA BOUQUET — To please a lover or to climb the ladder of success requires only the desire, according to Lord Chesterfield's Letters to His Son.

This oil may assist you in doing either. Place a drop on the wrists, back of the knees, and nape of the neck after the bath. Then, whether your objectives are in relation to business or romance, little or no resistance should be encountered.

INDIAN GUIDE — Aids in drawing a Guide for protection, assistance, numbers, and secret messages. Can be placed in an open dish in any room.

INFLAMMATORY CONFUSION — A scent dedicated to inciting turmoil, stress, and ill will among those within its subtle sensory stimulus. Where there is an open bottle placed in a room friction, dissension, and arguments will soon arise.

To break up a pair of lovers, place a drop on each person's clothing.

INFLUENCE — Use this when presenting your point of view on any subject — when asking for a raise, borrowing money, requesting a favor, or trying to convince another to your way of thinking. Apply to the temples and throat to clarify your thoughts and loosen your tongue.

INVISIBLE — The best kept secret in all of magic — how to make oneself invisible in order to gain entrance to buildings or eavesdrop on others without being seen — and there is no "instant magic" that will make you disappear as it takes years of intense study to learn this feat. However, this oil is the next best thing as it has such a soothing, lulling, quieting aroma that you can wear it anywhere without attracting undue attention from those around you.

IRRESISTIBLE — As the name suggests, this scent is reputed to make the one who wears this so attractive and beguiling that no one he or she meets can prevail against their suggestions, invitations, or advances.

ISIS — The ancient Egyptian Goddess of Love probably wore a similar fragrance and she was so powerful that she restored life to Osiris and to her son Horus. For the modern woman who wishes to be both woman and goddess, faithful and loving wife, or tender and devoted mother, try this spellbinding oil. It is a worthy fragrance called by the name of Isis who was, among other titles, called, "the queen of all gods," "the light-giver of heaven," and "lady of abundance."

J

JAMAICA — From the enchanted West Indies Island comes this magical fragrance which can add life and excitement and romance to anyone who sprinkles this freely around the home and on the body.

To restore pep and energy to a weary body, add to the bath water and soak in it for ten minutes or more. Come out of the tub revitalized and feeling years younger.

JAPANESE — Wear this perfume and be visited by the Seven Gods of Luck — Bishamon who rules over war and victory, Ebisu for fisherman's luck, Fukurokujin for the gift of prophesy and for miracles, Daikoku who confers wealth and happiness, Benten for talent in art and literature, Hotei for wisdom, and Jurojin for longevity.

JASMINE — A sacred flower in ancient Persia, the oil made from this climbing shrub with the extremely sweet-scented flowers is said to attract a great variety of good spirits toward the wearer.

A really powerful love spell to bind a person is done with this oil. To attract a lover, secure nine hairs from their head and place them in a bottle of this oil. Each day, for nine successive days, take one hair from the oil and burn it as you repeat this chant to Oshun, the African goddess of love, marriage, and gold:

> Oshun, Oshun, is your mirror clear?
> Look and see what I have here.
> It's hair off the head of one unwed
> Make him (of her) alone my very own.

JEALOUSY — To arouse jealousy in another, write the person's name on parchment and place the paper beneath a brown candle on your table or altar. Anoint the candle with this potent oil. As you light the candle, concentrate on the person and think strongly of doubt, uncertainty, confusion, and envy. Conduct this ritual each Monday and Friday for three weeks. Burn the candle for fifteen minutes at each devotion, and while it is burning, read Psalm 70 several times.

JERUSALEM — Bring a shower of blessings upon your home with only a few drops sprinkled at each entrance once a week.

If gaining money and friends are your primary objectives, sprinkle on Sunday. For attracting love, Monday is preferred. Thursdays are favored when improved health is needed.

This small prayer accompanying the sprinkling can insure a serene and productive week ahead:

Bless this day, bless this week,
Look down on me from high above.
Grant me courage for I am weak;
Guard me and those I love.

JEZEBEL — A secret formula used by women who wish to have their way with any man, as it can cause males to do their bidding without question.

To dominate a man completely, secure from any place on his head or body some hairs. Also get some of his fingernail or toenail clippings. Place the hair and nails in a bottle of this oil and wrap the bottle in a piece of black cloth. Hide the bottle away so that the man will not find it. As long as the man is yielding to your wishes and submissive to your desires leave the bottle in its secret place. But if the time comes when he becomes rebellious or defiant, shake the bottle vigorously several times to regain control of the situation.

A Seal of Arielis is designed to compel others to do one's bidding, and the Jezebel Oil applied to it weekly greatly adds to its power.

JINX — Formulated not to harm, but to protect from the evil intentions of those who may wish to damage your property or person.

For safe-keeping at all times, apply it to the soles of the feet after the morning bath or shower. Accompany the anointing with your own or this simple petition:

Make happy this day, I humbly pray,
Keep from it every destructive force.

Bring favor to the work I do this day,
And lend me strength to stay the course.

JINX KILLER — Should one become convinced that a destructive force has descended on their home or person, it is this formula which could bring quick relief.

Purchase the largest black candle possible, and a talisman from the Sixth & Seventh Books of Moses known as the Seal of Mephistophilas. This is a design to aid in overcoming and controlling one's enemies and protects from the plots of foes.

Place the seal beneath the candle after applying a drop of oil to each corner. As each drop is applied, pray sincerely this prayer composed by John Greenleaf Whittier over a hundred years ago:

Dear Lord and Father of mankind,
Forgive our foolish ways!
Reclothe us in our rightful mind,
In purer lives Thy service find,
In deeper reverence, praise.
Drop Thy still dews of quietness,
Till all our strivings cease;
Take from our souls the strain and stress,
And let our ordered lives confess
The beauty of Thy peace.

Light the candle and burn for one hour. Then extinguish the flame, repeating the prayer given.

Repeat daily until the situation is improved.

JINX REMOVING — For all those in a crossed condition, rub on the temples every day until the situation is improved.

For a stubborn hex which has been hanging around too long, get a voodoo doll (any doll will do as long as it is a bright color) and make two tags, one for the front and one for the back of the doll. Write your name on the tags and tie or pin them onto the doll securely. Soak the doll overnight in a solution of Four Thieves Vinegar and Water — half of each. The next morning lay the doll out to dry, preferably in the sunshine. When it is thoroughly dry, place the doll on a piece of white cloth, preferably a piece of your own clothing. Pour the full bottle of the Jinx Removing Oil over the doll and wrap it in the cloth or clothing. Go at once and bury the doll in the ground, chanting as you cover the doll with dirt:

Here is (insert your name), jinx, come on in,
Let's have fun and let's have sin,
Here in the ground, jinx, come on in,
We'll stay here through thick and thin.

The spell will leave your real body and settle into its grave with the doll which now represents you. Keep the grave sprinkled with the oil once a week to remain free of the jinx which was placed upon you.

JOB — This is just the perfume you ought to wear to help you find a job or to keep the one you've got.

When seeking employment, put a lodestone in a red flannel bag and feed it weekly with magnetic sand. Place also in the bag a Seal of the Air, called by some the Seal of Relief from Want, and anoint the bag daily with Job Oil until work is found.

JOCKEY CLUB — This can be used to anoint any charm bag. It is said to bring good results when letters are anointed with this before being sent or mailed.

For uncrossing purposes, dab at the base of the throat morning and night.

JOHN THE CONQUEROR — Probably the most popular of all the occult oils, it is believed to aid the wearer in all his endeavors. Promotes agile mental abilities and quick, clear thinking.

It is added to incenses to increase their vibrations, and on mojo bags to intensify their potency. Candles are anointed with it and it can be added to the bath water. Claims of its effectiveness in bringing to the user victory over all odds are legendary.

JOY — Formulated from legendary Hindu, Arabian, and Egyptian botanicals, this essence brings out the best in the wearer; talents are increased, one's thoughts become more optimistic, and one's body seems to attract pleasure. If one is depressed and lonely, this can change one's whole attitude, and hence one's entire life. Become betwitching with the delightful aroma of Joy Oil.

JU JU — Often called African Ju Ju Oil. An extremely potent enticement when worn as a perfume, said to make the user alluring, betwitching, and seductive. It is also a protective oil, guarding the wearer from hexes attempted by others.

JUDGE BE FOR ME — Just before entering the courtroom where your case is to be heard, rub the wrists with this powerful fragrance which can turn things in your favor. As you apply the oil, chant confidently:

>My cause is truly just,
>This you will surely see.
>I beg for simple trust
>And that justice be with me.

JUNGLE QUEEN — Believed to bring out the primitive in men and in women. Either sex can wear it on ear lobes to heighten sensual pleasure and unrestrained affection.

JUPITER — Among the Greek-Roman gods, Jupiter represents the supreme virtues of the judgment and the will. This oil is prepared for use by those who wish to acquire riches, protection from all earthly dangers, win honors and glory, and gain tranquility of mind.

JURY WINNING — When faced with court proceedings, it can be

advantageous to copy Psalm 20 with Dove's Blood Ink onto parchment paper. Take the talisman to court each day, anointing the corners just before court begins with this powerful fragrance which can turn the wheels of justice in your favor.

1. The Lord hear thee in the day of trouble; the name of the God of Jacob defend thee;

2. Send thee help from the sanctuary, and strengthen thee out of Zion;

3. Remember all thy offerings, and accept thy burnt sacrifice. Selah.

4. Grant thee according to thine own heart, and fulfill all thy counsel.

5. We will rejoice in thy salvation, and in the name of our God we will set up our banners; the Lord fulfill all thy petitions.

6. Now know I that the Lord saveth his anointed; He will hear him from his holy heaven with the saving strength of his right hand.

7. Some trust in chariots, and some in horses, but we will remember the name of the Lord our God.

8. They are brought down and fallen, but we are risen, and stand upright.

9. Save, Lord; let the king hear us when we call.

JUST JUDGE — This is worn to court when justice is in the balance and mercy is needed to tip the scales in your favor. Add it to the bath water on the morning of the trial or appearance, and also rub on arms, neck, and bosom.

Before signing any papers or documents which have to be presented to the court, rub the Just Judge Oil on the fingertips.

K

KEEP AWAY ENEMIES — Protect your person and property with this shielding scent. Sprinkle across all doorways and wipe onto all windowsills once a week. Anoint a sachet with the oil and hang it in your clothes closet.

On awakening each morning, pray the first four verses of Psalm 27:

1. The Lord is my light and my salvation; whom shall I fear? The Lord is the strength of my life; of whom shall I be afraid?

2. When the wicked, even mine enemies and my foes, came upon me to eat up my flesh, they stumbled and fell.

3. Though a host should encamp against me, my heart shall not fear: though war should rise against me, in this will I be confident.

4. One thing have I desired of the Lord, that will I seek after; that I may dwell in the house of the Lord all the days of my life, to behold the beauty of the Lord, and to inquire in his temple.

KEEP AWAY EVIL — To free the home of sinister forces, sprinkle three drops of this scent every third day at each of the entrances to the premises. Chant at each anointing this affirmation three times:

Thou knowest what is best;
And who but Thee, O God, hath power to know?
In Thy great will my trusting heart shall rest;
Beneath that will my humble head shall bow.
Trust confidently that all — home, family, possessions — will be protected.

KEEP AWAY HATE — It is far better to pardon than to resent. Forgiveness eliminates the expense of anger, the destruction of
hatred, and the waste of serenity.

Rub the oil on the temples and pray sincerely St. Francis'
prayer which will quickly bring release from the bondage of
bitterness:

> Lord, make me an instrument of Thy peace.
> Where there is hate, may I bring love;
> Where offense, may I bring pardon;
> May I bring union in place of discord;
> Truth, replacing error;
> Faith, where once there was doubt;
> Hope, for despair;
> Light, where was darkness;
> Joy to replace sadness.
> Make me not to so crave to be loved as to love.
> Help me to learn that in giving I may receive;
> In forgetting self, I may find life eternal.

KEEP AWAY TROUBLE — To be certain that all adversity is
cleared from the premises, use the Jinx Removing Wash to
scrub all windowsills and the entranceways.

Then apply a few drops of the oil to these same places,
praying with each application Psalm 91, Verses 5 through 11:

> Thou shalt not be afraid for the terror by night;
> nor for the arrow that flieth by day;
> Nor for the pestilence that walketh in darkness;
> nor for the destruction that wasteth at noon-
>   day.
> A thousand shall fall at thy side,
> and ten thousand at thy right hand;
> but it shall not come nigh thee.
> Only with thine eyes shall thou behold
> and see the reward of the wicked.
> Because thou has made the Lord,
> which is my refuge, even the most high,
> thy habitation.

There shall no evil befall thee,
neither shall any plague come nigh thy dwell-
ing.
For he shall give his angels charge over thee,
to keep thee in all thy ways.

For continued confidence, repeat the ritual once a week, preferably every Sunday.

KEEP ME — A beguiling scent for use when one needs a friend, relative — or even a stranger — to grant favors, loan or give money, or perform a service.

Apply the oil to your own right palm and, as quickly as possible thereafter, shake hands firmly with the one who has the power to meet your requests for assistance.

State your needs as simply and briefly as possible, along with your intention to repay the favor in kind as soon as your circumstances have improved.

KINDLY SPIRIT — To summon an unearthly being to your side for aid in accomplishing your tasks, write your requirement on parchment paper and place the petition beneath a pink candle.

Anoint the candle only from the center to the base, chanting as you apply the oil.

Guide my feet, guard my way,
Bless all I meet this day.
Bring to me the knowledge I need,
I will follow, faith will I lead.

KING SOLOMON — Used on the forehead to make one able to commune with the infinite and draw upon it for tremendous wisdom and power.

To draw prosperity to your house, keep a Seal of Fortune from the Sixth and Seventh Books of Moses under a green or Prosperity Brand candle in your home. Anoint it with the oil and burn it for one hour each day along with a mixture of Fast Luck and Helping Hand Incense.

KLUDDE — This oil, named for an evil goblin who is able to transform himself into any animal, protects one from the dangers of vicious dogs, predators of all kinds — human and animal, slithering snakes, stinging bees, and all other four-footed foes.

KNOWLEDGE — To be able to understand and put to use all that one hears or reads, apply a drop to the temples and back of the neck each morning after the bath or shower. As soon as convenient, sit and pray sincerely Verse 3 from Jeremiah, Chapter 33, wherein the Lord promises enlightenment to all who ask.

> Call unto me, and I will answer thee,
> and will tell you great and hidden things
> which you have not known.

KYPHI — This name was probably derived from Kypris, the Cypriot goddess of love — and analogous to the Greek goddess of love, beauty, generation and fertility, Aphrodite.

Use as a perfume, particularly at the nape of the neck and on the ear lobes, when one is interested in attracting a love partner.

L

LA FLAMME — Women wear this seductive scent when attempting to ensnare an unwilling man. The message will reach his heart quickly when the lady uses The Flame as her perfume.

LADY LUCK — For good fortune to smile on your cards, numbers, or horse, be sure the money you wager is rubbed with this oil before placing the bet. It can also be used as a perfume or rubbed on the back of the hands when playing games of chance.

LAVENDER — As far back as the 16th Century, lavender was placed between the bed sheets to prevent moths, and many modern homes still use it in their closets for this purpose and to keep the linens fresh and fragrant.

To encourage thrift and prudence in all matters, anoint the wrists, throat, and ankles daily.

To promote peace in the home, add it to your scrub water weekly or keep an open bottle on the table, mantel, or other convenient place.

If you feel that someone is trying to take your job from you, discredit you with the boss, or in any way interfere with your work, write that person's name on a square of parchment and place it in a red flannel bag along with some cumin seed and some devil's shoestring herb. Place the bag in a safe place and anoint it daily with Lavender Oil so that the person will become very involved in his own affairs and will leave you completely alone.

LAW STAY AWAY — Should the occasion arise when you particularly do not want your home or automobile inspected by the police, mix ten drops of oil into your regular scrubbing solution. As you wash the area you wish protected, chant softly this anonymous verse:

> Faithfully faithful to every trust,
> Honestly honest in every deed,
> Righteously righteous and justly just,
> This is the whole of a good man's creed.

LEMON — Used by mediums as an aid in calling the spirits as lemon is a favorite of many spiritual beings.

To entice protective spirits into the home, mix with any incense you may be using.

LEMON GRASS — A formula believed to aid the development of one's psychic senses is used by many mediums, spiritualists, and psychics.

Apply to the wrists, ankles, and around the neckline.

Carry on your person a talisman from the 18th century grimoire, The Black Pullet, which bestows onto the possessor the power to read the thoughts of all persons. When it becomes advantageous to know the contemplation of another, apply the oil to the temples and around the neckline. Sit in a relaxed position in a comfortable chair and, holding the talisman between the palms of both hands, concentrate on the subject's thoughts. Close the eyes, relax, and within a few minutes — sometimes only seconds — you will be absorbing vibrations, words, and even pictures of the thoughts of others.

LEO (July 23 to August 22) — Sun is the ruling planet. The House of Determination. Lucky day is Sunday. Lucky numbers are 2 and 7. Your special perfume will help you keep the active mind, good nature, and enthusiasm (which are the qualities all Leos possess) working for you and help ease any disappointments you may encounter.

LIBRA (September 23 to October 22) — Venus is the ruling planet. The House of Partnership and Justice. Lucky day is Friday. Lucky numbers are 6 and 9. Libras are generally generous, passionate, and adventurous, fond of excitement, travel, and change, so their special scent is prepared to help them keep a more even keel between their extreme happiness and abject downheartedness. Libras also usually lack order in both their homes and their lives, and this perfume can help provide the stability and determination they need to get a job done.

LIFE — A healing oil to be used when the medical doctor has either been unable to treat successfully or when no organic reason for the condition can be found. Apply to the affected part of the body and repeat this prayer with great faith, "Grant your servant, O Lord, health of mind and body. Let me be delivered from my burden and my sorrow, and grant me the blessings of present joy and eternal happiness in Thy kingdom."

The Oil of Life is used by all believers in its powers to insure good health and a long life.

LILAC — Anoint the back of the neck to improve the memory and to draw many good spirits.

One of the good spirits who may be susceptible to this fragrance is Bael who confers upon the petitioner the needed wisdom to assist one in making the correct decision when faced with seemingly unsurmountable problems. Draw (it's pictured in the Lesser Key of Solomon book) or purchase from an occult supply house a Seal of Bael and anoint the edges with Lilac Oil. Hold it in the palms of the hands held closely together as you ponder the problem which concerns you. The best way to deal with the situation should come to you as you consider the various alternatives you have to choose from.

LILY OF THE VALLEY — This scent was once considered so precious that only vessels of gold were considered fit to contain it. It is an appropriate oil for anointing any sacred objects, and may be worn as a perfume by all who appreciate its lovely fragrance.

A quieting agent, said to be very soothing and calming to the nerves. Use on the back of the neck and on the forehead of one who is emotionally upset to bring peace and serenity.

LIME — Apply two drops to love incense and burn once a week to keep a lover faithful and loyal. Dress a pink candle with Lime Oil and burn for the same purpose. In either case, write the loved one's name on parchment and place it beneath the incense burner or candle holder before the incense or candle is lighted.

LINDEN — This is a love oil when it is worn as a perfume to draw friendships.

It is a healing oil when it is rubbed across the stomach

and shoulder blades, soothing aches and pains, and restoring strength and energy to the body. Apply the oil, repeat the 146th Psalm, lie down and rest for one-half hour. Then arise and see if you cannot feel almost immediately the curative effects.

LODESTONE — See Lucky Lodestone Oil. The uses are similar, so experiment with both formulas and decide for yourself which fragrance you prefer.

LOOK ME OVER — An attention attracting oil. Use sparingly but with confidence that it will enable you to project a kind and friendly attitude which will cause all you meet to regard you with interest and pleasure.

LOST AND AWAY — A banishing blend used to rid one's home of unwelcome visitors. Sprinkle a few drops onto the intruder's clothes, into their suitcase, or on the soles of the unwanted one's shoes. Repeat the anointing every third day until the desired results are obtained.

LOTTERY — Combined in this formula are elements for good fortune, money drawing, and gambling luck — a truly odds-in-your-favor combination!

Anoint the four corners of your tickets as you chant at each point:

> Lucky, lucky I will be,
> Lots of money I do see.
> Come my way this very day.

LOTUS — A sacred flower in the Far East, it has high spiritual connotations, and was once closely associated with Egyptian magical rites.

It is believed that the woman who uses this has her way with any man as it is impossible for him to refuse her requests.

To win the love of a man, get a red candle in the shape of a male figure. Rub the Lotus Oil all over the surface of the image. Write the man's name on parchment and place the paper beneath the candle. Stick a pin into the candle in the region of the heart, light the candle and repeat:

Love come over thee, Love overcome thee,
Love for (your name), love for me.

Let the candle burn completely and all the man's resistance to you will be destroyed.

LOVE OR LOVERS — These are usually the same oil, just a variation of the name used by different dealers. It is used on the body by both parties and can allegedly bind the two sweethearts together so that neither friend nor foe can drive them apart.

To keep a loved one true, anoint a red candle with a mixture of Love and Controlling oils. Beneath the candle place a square of parchment on which you have written your own and your lover's name. After sunset, burn some Fire of Love Incense, and light the candle. Burn for ten minutes. Repeat the ritual each evening until your love is secure.

LOVE BREAKER — Be careful when using this — if you get it on your own hands or clothes, wash thoroughly with strong soap to remove it quickly. It is used to break up another's marriage or affairs, and should be applied to the clothing of both persons involved.

LOVE DRAWING — Anoint the corners of a Table of Venus Seal, the planet which relates to love, and assists in all matters of the heart — with marriage, partnerships, social affairs, and friendly relationships. Do this every Friday, the day for ceremonies of love, lust, pleasure and friendship.

If the attraction of a particular person is the object of the spell, write his or her name with Dove's Blood Ink on the reverse before the oil is applied. Carry the talisman in purse or pocket until the mission is accomplished.

LOVE DROPS — Used to make the one you love want to be ever near you. Best when applied to the Love Centers — back of ears, base of the neck, and beneath the breasts.

LOVE ME — Entice the reluctant object of your affections by wearing this fragrance as a perfume and secretly applying a drop of the same oil to the loved one's clothing or body. Do not expect immediate results but persistence should result in a romantic liaison with the one you desire.

LOVERS — See under Love.

LUCIFER — A hexing mixture which is said to bring aches and pains to the part of the body to which it is applied. Strong, so use sparingly.

To place a curse on an enemy, write his (or her) name on parchment with Dragon's Blood Ink. Place the paper at the bottom of an incense burner and cover it with Lucifer Incense. On top of the incense, sprinkle nine drops of the oil. Light the incense at midnight. Repeat the ritual for nine consecutive nights, and thereafter once a week to keep the foe hexed.

LUCK IN A HURRY — When Lady Luck seems to have moved out of your neighborhood, entice her back quickly. This is a particularly potent concoction which may bring results far beyond one's hopes or expectations.

Anoint the entrances to the home and, as you apply the oil, chant three times at each point:

Hurry, good fortune, come this way
Enter and stay a while with me.
You are welcome, each and every day
Settle here for a spell, do not flee.

LUCKY BUSINESS — Place a green candle near the entrance to your shop, anoint it with the oil, and burn during business hours. Just before opening the doors to allow customers to enter, anoint the threshold also with several drops of the oil, chanting as you sprinkle the fragrance:

> Enough I ask to fill the soul,
> Then a bit of overflow;
> Enough for substance in my bowl,
> And a bit more income than outgo.

LUCKY DICE — When playing games of chance with dice, it can be most fortunate if they are dipped in or sprinkled with this gambling scent. If it is not possible to anoint the dice, then rub the oil into the palms of the hand before the game begins.

LUCKY DOG — A favorite of gamblers who believe it attracts favorable vibrations. Used to anoint Southern John Roots — seven drops once a week is said to keep it healthy and active.

LUCKY HAND — One of the most popular of the "good luck" concoctions, believed to bring luck, love, power, success, and protection.

During times of distress, ease the burden by securing a seven-layer candle which has seven different colors. Dress it thoroughly with the oil and burn one layer each day for seven consecutive days. As each layer of the candle melts, into your home will come a corresponding blessing — love, health, peace, plenty, happiness, virtue, long life. If a seven-layer candle is not available, use seven white candles, placing a label for each blessing underneath each candle and proceed with the ritual.

LUCKY LADY — See Lady Luck Oil.

LUCKY LODESTONE — For anointing magnetic lodestones, or wear as an excellent oil for developing good fortune and changing bad luck to good.

To help make good decisions, take a magnetic lodestone and anoint it with oil. Wrap around the stone a Master Key Seal from the Sixth and Seventh Books of Moses and carry it in the purse or pocket in a red flannel bag. Place in the bag also the problem you are trying to solve or the question you want answered (this is to be written on a piece of parchment). Dress the bag with the Lucky Lodestone Oil daily and carry the bag with you. Within three days your solution or answer should become clear to you.

LUCKY LOTTERY — A specially prepared scent for anointing tickets to increase their chance of winning. As you place a drop at each corner, chant this little rhyme:

> Lucky I am, a big win I see,
> Fortune is mine, it's sure to be.
> Hundreds, thousands, maybe more,
> It will come pouring in my door.

LUCKY MOJO — Similar to Mojo or Wishing oil, but this is formulated with extra strength so that it reputedly is successful where the others have failed.

When you have a particular objective in mind, write the desire on a square of parchment paper. Apply a drop of oil to each corner and then roll the talisman into a cylinder, tying it with white ribbon so that it is secure. Place the charm in a small bottle or jar. Put a secure lid on the container, wrap it in a clean white cloth, and secrete it in a safe place.

Every third day, take the container out, undo the lid, unwrap the cloth, and chant three times while holding the talisman between the palms of one's hands:

> This petition I ask to be,
> It is my heart's desire.
> It doth bring harm to none,
> Fulfillment only good will inspire.

LUCKY MONTH — Similar to the astrological oils, this is formulated to attract good fortune during a certain period of time. This can be used by all — no matter when your birthday falls.

It is believed by many that a drop a day — on the wrists, sole of the foot, or at the nape of the neck — applied each morning after the bath, will keep one safe and free from harm all day.

LUCKY NUMBER — When purchasing lottery tickets, choosing a bingo card, or selecting a number of any kind for gambling purposes, anoint the finger tips of both hands before the ticket, card, or number is chosen.

> After the selection is in hand, chant several
> times silently:
> All is quiet, all is calm,
> Such good fortune in my palm.
> Lucky is my true good friend,
> And will be until the end.

LUCKY NINE — Nine drops in the bath should bring success if you are looking for a job. Anointing the crown of the head for nine consecutive nights should help all who are in financial trouble.

The Hebrews regarded nine as the symbol of truth, it also represents force and energy. Use the Lucky Nine Oil as your special perfume whenever you lack the vitality or fortitude you need.

LUCKY PLANET — Used to draw the vibrations of a favorable planet to you. A mixture made up of those particular ingredients specified for the various planetary oils — Sun, Moon, Mercury, Venus, Jupiter, Mars, and Saturn — this is a good all-purpose oil concocted to draw from the planets their powers for good and direct them toward the aims and projects of the wearer.

LUCKY PLAY — Used in all forms of gambling and games of

chance. When applied to the body as a perfume, it is reputedly a highly magnetic attracting agent which can tilt the odds to favor the one who wears this.

It may also enhance one's chances when playing bingo or lottery if the oil is rubbed on the edge of the cards or tickets.

LUCKY PROFIT — Keep a small vial of this in the cash register or money drawer. Each morning, before opening for business, rub the bottom and sides of the money tray.

It may also be advantageous to sprinkle a few drops across the entrance way to the place of business just before opening the door to customers.

LUCKY PROPHET — This is a formula which can activate inborn clairvoyant powers so that this gift can be developed to one's full potential. Most authorities believe these talents are natural to all of us, simply lying dormant until they are either needed or desired.

To attempt to view future happenings, dim all lights in the room. The quieter the surroundings, the better the chances of enlightening messages to unveil the events to come. Very soft background music (without vocals) of a soothing nature can be helpful toward calming and clearing the mind of extraneous noises and thoughts.

Anoint the forehead and back of the neck with the oil. Sit in a comfortable position or lie flat on the back on a sofa or bed. Close the eyes and relax, concentrating only on the quiet or the soothing music.

Wait for at least ten minutes (but do not watch the clock or try to be conscious of time) for a message or a vision to come into the subconscious. It is normal if you should fall asleep. When you awaken, stay quiet and serene for a few more minutes in the event that there are further revelations or messages.

If no communication comes, this is not unusual and do

not despair. Wait three days minimum, and then repeat the procedure. Success usually comes by the third or fourth attempt. If not, keep trying for the results will be worth the effort.

LUCKY SEVEN — A general, potent luck drawing scent — dedicated toward attracting good fortune every day of the week.

Apply to the soles of the feet each morning after the bath so that your steps may be directed toward good fortune as you go about your daily tasks.

LUCKY SWEEPSTAKE — A potent gambler's oil; use it on the racing form, the bingo card, lottery ticket, etc.

One of the Seals from The Black Pullet, a late 18th Century publication about black magic, called the Brings Good Fortune talisman, should be bound onto the left forearm with red ribbon whenever you gamble. Touch it with the right forefinger before placing each wager — but do not attract the notice of your opponents.

LUCKY 13 — Take away all the unfavorable implications of thirteen with this oil which should eliminate the negative and accentuate the positive aspects of your life.

For good fortune in your home, dress a purple candle with the Lucky 13 Oil and burn it fifteen minutes every day.

LUCKY WIN — To add power and draw fortunate vibrations to your lottery ticket, bingo card, or other gambling document, copy Verses 15 and 16 of Psalm 74 onto a piece of parchment paper, using the Dove's Blood Ink:

> Thou didst cleave the fountain and the flood,
> thou driest up mighty rivers.
> The day is thine, the night also is thine;
> thou hast prepared the light and the sun.

Roll the charm into a cylinder shape and tie it with red cord, string, or ribbon which has been saturated with the oil. Keep the talisman in a secret place until the results of your wager are known and then destroy it for it should be only used once.

LUV, LUV, LUV — An extraordinary oil, specially formulated to attract to the one who wears this those already involved or attached to another.

A very effective separating spell can be done with three candles, two red and one white. First, the candles are identified by writing on parchment the names of those in the triangle — your own, the one you wish to come to you, and the one who is presently involved with the one you desire. Under the two red candles place the name of the one you want for yourself, and the "other woman" or "other man" in the situation. Under the white candle, place your own name. Leave the "other person's" candle undressed, but anoint the other red and your white candle with the oil. Place the two red candles side by side and place the white candle apart from them, at least a foot or more. Light all three candles each day and burn them for fifteen minutes. Each time you light the candles, move the candle of the one you wish to come to you a little closer to your white candle. By the seventh day, the "other person's" candle will be standing alone — as he or she probably really will be in life — and you and your loved one will be together.

LYANG LYANG — An alluring magnetic essence formulated to make the wearer irresistible. Use in the bath and as a perfume.

MAD — Sprinkle in a room or across the doorway to cause tension, hard feelings, anxiety, and stress to those who enter the premises.

To cause pain or distress in a particular part of an enemy's body, secure a corresponding part of an animal — bone, heart, eye, liver, brains, ribs. Attach to the animal part a tag with your foe's name on it. Place the part in a small box, and as you sprinkle on it the Mad oil, repeat this curse nine times:

> (Name of enemy), I call upon the powers that be,
> To seize you now and cause you pain,
> To hold you till you scream in anguish.
> Through hot and cold, and sun and rain,
> You'll hurt like hell, this I wish.

Bury the box and sprinkle the grave once a week with the oil to keep the foe in constant torment.

MAGIC — When all else has failed, try this. It may be just the thing needed to turn your impossible objective into a reality. Use it in the bath water, or as a perfume.

To find the answer to a perplexing problem, prepare a small rounded bowl of clear water. Concentrate on your dilemma as you sprinkle thirteen drops of the oil onto the water. Then, with the right index finger slowly stir the bowl of water, making one circle clockwise, then one circle counter clockwise, thirteen times, repeating this chant with each circle:

> For every evil under the sun,
> There is a remedy, or there is none!
> If there be one, try to find it,
> If there be none, never mind it!

A remedy, solution or answer should come to you shortly thereafter.

MAGNET — An oil for many purposes. Wear to magnetize others toward you. Dress lodestones with it or anoint John the Conqueror roots to draw business and good luck.

When attending the races make your own personal lucky talisman by drawing on a square of parchment a horseshoe. Place the paper horseshoe and a lodestone in your red flannel bag, and anoint the bag with the Magnet Oil before you leave home. Touch the bag with the fingers each time you pick a horse.

MAGNOLIA — Recommended as an aid in psychic development when the head is anointed.

To locate lost or misplaced items, secure a Seal of Treasures (which design is from the Sixth and Seventh Books of Moses book) and anoint each corner of it with the oil. Carry it in your purse or pocket for seven days, and before the week is up, your lost, misplaced, or even stolen goods will have been found or returned to you.

MANDRAKE — This oil, sometimes offered with a bit of the Mandagora in it, is used with incense or rubbed on candles to give them added powers for protection. It is also used in hexing spells and for anointing voodoo dolls.

To prepare a particularly lethal spell to bring harm to an enemy, get a black voodoo doll and attach to it a tag with the foe's name written on it. Soak the doll overnight in this oil, and at sunrise take the doll to the enemy's home and nail it to the north side of his house.

MANPOWER — Need the vigor, vitality, and energy necessary for lasting lovepower? The Force you are lacking may be found in this oil which should be applied to the hips and thighs each evening before retiring. Try it, and you may be amazed at the change from apathy to ability in just a few weeks.

MAN TRAP — If you always seem to be the one who loses out to others in the search for the man of your dreams, reinforce your efforts by wearing this rejuvenating aroma whenever you go out in quest of your personal Don Juan.

MARRIAGE — For those who are trying to convince a lover to tie the nuptial knot, this oil should be rubbed into the hairline of the loved one; all round the head. Their thoughts will be of no one else until the union is made binding.

To bind a husband, wife, or lover close within the circle of love which you desire for the two of you, take a photograph of the two of you together (or two photographs of you and the loved one which have been taken separately) and place the picture on the table. Secure a length of red string, cord, yarn, or thin strip of cloth, about 20 inches long, or long enough to encircle the photos you have placed on the table. On the first day of the ritual, make a knot in the string, about three inches from one end, dip the knot in the oil, and repeat three times quickly:

> With this knot I bind thee to me,
> Faithful forever thee will be.

Continue the ritual tying of the knot daily, placing each knot an inch or two apart from the one made the day before. When the knots reach close to the end of the string, on the final day tie the two ends of the string together in a knot, and repeat three times quickly:

> These (say how many) knots have bound you
>   to me,
> As faithful as I to you, so faithful to me you'll be.

Place the string of knots around the photograph and leave it undisturbed, anointing it once weekly to keep your love circle intact.

MARS — Men particularly like this oil as it adds to their energy, virility, and passion.

Both men and women use it liberally on the wrists and hands when facing any foe to acquire courage.

Soldiers who believe it leads to military honors favor it.

To cause ruin, discord, and hostility amongst one's enemies, sprinkle it in their home or rub it on their clothes.

MASTER OR MASTERS — One of the most powerful occult oils. Many uses.

Five drops in the bath water is used to keep all evil away.

Sprinkled on the body it is believed to attract friends.

When looking for work, rub some on heels and base of hands.

MASTER KEY — Carry with you a replica of the Master Key talisman from the Sixth & Seventh Books of Moses so that you will be assured of good health, good fortune, and success in your personal and business affairs. Anoint the edges of the seal weekly for uninterrupted benefits.

MEDITATION — This carries a strong mystical aura and should be used only while meditating, praying, or doing psychic work. Anoint the altar and altar cloths with it, and apply to the forehead in the shape of a cross, bringing the first stroke downward toward the nose, then across from temple to temple. When applying the oil, say Psalm 135 devoutly.

MEMORY DROPS — Also called Memory Oil. Believed to improve the mental processes, helping students to pass tests, aiding in the remembering of names, numbers, and assisting in locating lost articles. Anoint the forehead and temples once an hour until the objective is accomplished.

MERCURY — Use on the forehead when meditating to gain answers to questions and to foresee the future.

Mercury governs all communications so use it when speaking before others so they will heed your words. Anoint letters with it and you may be sure your writing will get a quick reply and good results.

MEXICAN LUCK — An enchanting perfume used by many to attract fame, fortune, or love.

MIDNIGHT — As a perfume, it is a powerful love oil. Also said to produce prophetic dreams if sprinkled on one's pillow.

To punish a person who has hurt you, secure a wax image in the shape of a man or woman, depending upon the one who has harmed you. Also secure a saucepan or other suitable container large enough to hold the image. Place in the pan an amount of water sufficient to cover the image which you place in the water. Liberally sprinkle in the water some of the Midnight Oil. Place the container on the stove and heat the water until the image is melted and no recognizable features remain. Then bury the entire container in the ground, cover it, and sprinkle the grave with the oil. That person will have no power to hurt you ever again.

MILLIONAIRE — If you want to be one — and are willing to take the necessary steps to gain that goal — start with the following prosperity chant each morning and anoint the temples with a drop of oil:

> For silver and gold, I now pray,
> Send me my needs, do not delay.
> More and more, I now request;
> For this reward I'll do my best.
> Piles of money at my feet,
> Oh, blessed be, it is so sweet.

MIMOSA — When one anoints the body with this just before retiring, it is believed to bring dreams which reveal coming events. This can be very useful when facing perplexing situations which require long-reaching decisions.

To have a vision during sleep of the one you will marry, just before bedtime, take a warm bath and add to the water at least nine drops of this oil. Soak for at least fifteen minutes. Then dry yourself and use more of the Mimosa Oil on the body. Get into bed and relax in a comfortable position. Be sure the room is dark and quiet. Gather all your mind's energy, blocking out all other thoughts, and rhythmically repeat this little chant until you fall asleep:

> As I sleep, I beg to see,
> The face of one who'll marry me.

MIND BENDER — When it is desired to have another person change their mind or opinion about you or some project in which you need their cooperation or assistance, use this fragrance.

It is recommended that the oil come into direct contact with the other person. This can be done in various ways.

Use as a lover's oil and anoint the partner's shoulders.

When this is done with gentleness and affection during love play, it almost always brings the results desired.

Should the help you need have to come from a stranger or casual acquaintance, place a drop or two on the stationery you use to write your request.

MINT — Similar to Spring Mint, it is both an energizer and a business enhancer.

Used as your regular perfume, it will bolster one's vigor and vitality.

Sprinkled at the entrance to a store; it can entice customers to come inside to view your wares.

MIRACLE — Should the situation become so oppressive, the tyranny so stifling, the load so heavy-laden, or the millstone so burdensome that you feel the breaking point approaching, lightly dampen a small towel with the oil and lie down. Place the fragrant cloth across the forehead and close the eyes. Visualize a small rippling brook, birds chirping, children's laughter as they wade in a pool, a spring scene of budding magnolia trees with its heady aroma, or a special personal memory of some magical scene in your own past.

It should be only a few minutes until you completely relax and possibly fall asleep. After this refreshing nap, you will awaken with new strength and determination, knowing that you are capable of facing the problem at hand and dealing with it in a serene, relaxed, and mature manner.

At this moment, pray this short poem entitled, "A Grateful Heart" by the 17th Century English clergyman and poet,

George Herbert:

> Thou has given so much to me,
> Give one thing more — a grateful heart;
> Not thankful when it pleaseth me,
> As if Thy blessings had spare days;
> But such a heart, whose pulse may be
> Thy praise.

MISTLETOE — For attracting customers, developing business, and drawing purchasers or clients, always have this in your place of business. The actual merchandise can be anointed if feasible, or sprinkle across the doorway where patrons are invited to enter. A few drops added to the scrub water once a week practically assures brisk traffic in the store and a full cash box by the end of the day.

MOJO — Or Wishing Oil. When you need a special favor or a wish to come true quickly, try this on throat, temples, and wrists.

If another person is involved in the fulfillment of your wish, obtain a First Pentacle of Saturn design which compels others to submit to your requests or desires. Anoint the talisman with the Mojo Oil at the four corners of the magic square which is within the outer circle of the design, and hold it between the palms as you make your wish.

MONEY DRAWING — Rub on the inside of the wallet each day, and anoint the four corners of all bills in one's possession once a week.

If one is in search of money, rub on the heels of both feet before leaving home.

To find cash, there is a special amulet which is to be made up and worn about the neck. Combine a teaspoon each of frankincense, saltpeter, Money Drawing Powder, and black snake root. Place this mixture in a chamois or leather bag, anoint it every morning with the Money Drawing Oil, and wear it until you have the necessary amount of money you need.

MONEY HOUSE BLESSING — To be rewarded with enrichments aplenty before the day is done, recite this small rhyme as you apply the oil to the nape of the neck and wrists each morning after the bath or shower:

> Fruit in the cupboard,
> Bread in the house,
> Money in the pocket,
> Love and friends hereabout.

MONEY MIST — Rub on the wallet to attract fantastic amounts of money and to protect the cash you have on hand.

MOON — Most of those people whose ruling planet is the moon like to travel, and this oil will protect you on your journey. Leave some open in the home while you are away so that it will be safeguarded in your absence.

It is a calming oil; soothing the emotional one, bringing sweet dreams during sleep, and softening bitterness toward others.

MOSES — Usually called the Oil of Moses, this is a holy oil, used during seances by those attempting to talk to the spirits in the other worlds, and for consecrating altars, utensils, and tools.

To protect the home, get a mezuzah which is a small case used by some Jewish families as a sign and reminder of their faith. Any small box or case will do, but the mezuzah is both convenient to use and attractive. Attach the mezuzah to the left top corner of doorpost, and inside it place a handwritten prayer on parchment. You can compose your own prayer, or use this one:

> Protect this home, I pray. Keep it safe through-
> out the day.
> Guard the house and all within. Make it free of
> vice and sin.

Before placing the prayer inside the mezuzah, anoint all edges of the parchment paper with the Oil of Moses. Thereafter anoint the prayer each Sunday at sunset.

MOTHER CHARITY — When in urgent need of financial assistance, anoint all the money in your possession — corners of all the bills and edges of the coins. Pray as you do this with the conviction that your crisis will be alleviated quickly:

> Blessed Mother,
> guide me, and be with me as this day I go
> about my daily tasks.
> May my efforts be rewarded,
> and my sins forgiven.
> Bless those I meet and, as I do unto them,
> may they in return do unto me.
> I ask Thy assistance in all I do
> this day which has been given me.
> Amen.

MOVING — So many are plagued with neighbors who cause trouble, disturbances, and tension to all those who live nearby. When the situation becomes too much to bear, sprinkle this oil on the property of the one you wish to become dissatisfied with the place where they live.

If you are a landlord and wish to get rid of an unruly tenant, or one who is not paying the rent, sprinkle the Moving Oil across the threshold of the apartment or house. After the premises are vacated, be sure to scrub well with the Jinx Removing Wash so that the oil will be removed.

Should you have an unwelcome guest in your home, add some of the oil to the water in which their clothes are washed, and within a very sort time the unwanted one will be packing those clothes and moving on to a new place and out of your life.

MUMMY — To catch a spirit and hold it captive so that it (the spirit of the person who is affecting you) cannot harm you or your property, transfer a small portion of the oil into a larger bottle — at lease three times larger than the oil's original container.

Add to the oil a whole Guinea Pepper, a few grains of sand, and a slip of paper on which you have scribed the name of your adversary with Dragon's Blood Ink. Seal the bottle and place it in a secret place. So long as the bottle remains undisturbed, so will the foe be unable to hurt, injure, or wrong you in any way.

MUSK — Use on hands and feet each morning to instill self-assurance, confidence, and strength. Especially useful when looking for work.

It is also a love oil as its aroma arouses ones passions and heightens sexual feelings.

MY DESIRE — Have a secret wish come true by scribing on parchment paper with Dove's Blood Ink the name of the person or object you desire to have as your own. Then fold the paper in this manner: top edge downward to a bit past the center, then left edge to center, right edge to center, and finally lower edge up to top. Tie the charm securely with red thread or ribbon and place it in a secret place where it will not be discovered by anyone else.

Every third day, anoint the talisman with three drops of oil, chanting with each drop this affirmation:

I bless this charm, I know my wish will be.
For all to see,
Blessed be this charm,
I know it is to be.
It will be fulfilled,
For all who wish to see.

Once the secret desire has come true, bury the talisman close to the entrance of the home.

MY MAN — Women use this in the belief that when the fragrance is sprinkled into a man's shoes, he will be unable to wander from home and family.

MYRRH — One of the gifts of the Magi to the Infant Jesus, myrrh is an ingredient in sacred ointments, incenses, and oils. As a powerful guard against any evil which may be directed toward one, anoint the temples each morning.

MYSTIC RITES — Often this oil can aid one in understanding those mysteries which seem to be beyond human comprehension.

Anoint the forehead and temples, sit quietly, meditating on the puzzle or problem at hand. Ponder on these few words from Hebrews II, Verse 1: "Faith is the substance of things hoped for, the evidence of things not seen." Before much time has past, some solution or answer to the quandry will come to mind.

MYSTIC VEIL — An ancient Indian formula based on a legend of substance which, when applied to the top of the head could change one's appearance to resemble anyone in existence, when rubbed on the temples would turn the eyes into a magic mirror, when walked upon a path where it was sprinkled would assure one of reaching his destination quickly and safely, and when the oil was placed in a shallow dish in a sickroom, any disease would be cured. Surely a most remarkable oil if even part of the legend is valid!

NARCISSUS — Wear on the body to bring calmness, harmony, and peace of mind. Dab a bit on the pillow to aid one toward tranquil sleep and sweet dreams of love.

NATURE — Place three drops in the bath water and lather the body all over well with a good quality Patchouli love soap. Wash thoroughly, rinse well and dress in fresh clean clothes. Do this daily and within a week, one can be rejuvenated with sufficient energy and vigor to fulfill any requirements one may be faced with in a sexual situation.

NEPTUNE — In primitive thought, Neptune was the god of heaven (that is, the god of clouds and of rain). Later he became the god of fresh water, and finally, he was seen as the god of the sea. It is he who unleashes storms — representing the passions of the soul — particularly in his most extreme role as the destroyer. This oil, when used daily and applied in a circle around the waistline of the body, should serve to calm the turbulence of these upheavals in one's life, particularly when they are caused by unleashed passion or rage.

NERVOUS — Any time you feel tense or anxious, add a few drops to a warm bath and soak for at least ten minutes. While in the tub, repeat this short prayer: "Sooth my troubled mind, quiet my jittery nerves, bring peace to my soul, and contentment to my life, so that I may go about my daily work with composure, tranquility, and serenity."

NEW LIFE — If one is bothered by past failures, guilts, or regrets, try this oil to help blot out the sad yesterdays of life. Use in the bath or as a perfume, and bear in mind that any time devoted to regrets for the past or fears of the future is lost from the only time we have — today.

If the home seems burdened with bad vibrations, get a blue candle for each room of the house. Anoint them with the New Life Oil and burn them all at the same time until they are consumed. It should clear the air of all negative forces.

NEW MONEY DROPS — Every seventh day, go through your purse or wallet and anoint the top edge of all your paper money, chanting as each bill is handled.

> One dollar, two dollar, five, ten,
> Bring more of each from where you've been.
> Ten dollar, five dollar, two, one.

Multiply, multiply, fore morning sun.

Repeat as needed so that your cash will grow steadily and you'll never be broke.

NEW ORLEANS — Legendary voodoo oil for attracting love, money, and good fortune.

NINE LUCKY MIXTURE — In Jesus' sermon on the mount, as related in the Book of Matthew, Chapter 5, Verses 3 through 11: "He blessed the poor in spirit, they that mourn, the meek, they which hunger and thirst after righteousness, the merciful, the pure in heart, the peacemakers, those falsely accused, and the persecuted."

This oil serves to bring untold blessings to those in need or despair when it is used daily to anoint the parchment upon which one has copied these Bible verses, and who reads them with reverence and a devout desire to improve one's circumstances:

Blessed are the poor,
for theirs is the kingdom of heaven.
Blessed are they that mourn,
for they shall be comforted.
Blessed are the meek,
for they shall inherit the earth.
Blessed are they which do hunger
and thirst after righteousness,
for they shall be filled.
Blessed are the merciful,
for they shall obtain mercy.
Blessed are the pure in heart,
for they shall see God.
Blessed are the peacemakers,
for they shall be called the children of God.
Blessed are they which are persecuted for
righteousness' sake,
for theirs is the kingdom of heaven.
Blessed are ye, when men shall revile you,

and persecute you,
and shall say all manner of evil against you
  falsely,
for my sake.

NINE MYSTERY — Composed of nine essences, this potent mixture is used to gain secret knowledge. Apply to the temples when you need to locate articles which are lost.

If you believe another person is withholding information, rub the oil on that person's throat to cause him to loosen his tongue and tell you what you want or need to know.

NIRVANA — Buddhists regard nirvana as the state of perfect blessedness achieved by the extinction of individual existence and by the absorption of the soul into the supreme being, or by the extinction of all desires and passions.

Should you feel you are losing control of your emotions of lust, passion, greed, obsession, gluttony, and such, let this fragrance control these detrimental feelings.

Whenever destructive thoughts enter the mind, write them briefly on paper. Roll the paper into a cylinder (pencil shape), tie it tightly with a white ribbon, and bury the talisman in a small freshly dug hole in the earth. Sprinkle it with oil, and fill in the dirt to cover the spot. Add a few drops of oil to the ground daily until you become confident in your power to ban injurious thoughts from the mind.

NOW OR NEVER — Should your patience become strained, a situation escalated into possible danger, or simply when you need immediate action taken in order to bring an end to a relationship which is no longer what you desire it to be, try easing the tension with this fast acting scent.

In just a few words write the problem on parchment. Rub the oil along all four edges of the paper — starting at the top left corner across to the right, downward on the right side, back along the bottom edge, and finally upward to connect with the upper left corner.

Fold the talisman in half, top to bottom, then left to right. Wrap red thread around it as many times as necessary to secure it in its folded form. Place the charm in a small empty box, anointing its edges each morning until results are attained.

NUMBER ONE — It really is okay not to be first in every objective you seek to obtain, but when you believe there is a real chance that you can "grab the gold ring", go for it! Bolster your courage and determination to compete with this energizing oil. Apply to the soles of the feet, inside the elbows, and back of the neck.

Chant at each anointing point this simple courage booster from the pen of Isaac Watts, 18th Century clergyman:

To heaven I lift my waiting eyes;
There all my hopes are laid;
The Lord that built the earth and skies
Is my perpetual aid.

NUTMEG — Upon awakening each morning, strengthen the senses by applying a dab at each temple. This can give one a sharper wit, clearer perception, and greater sensitivity.

OBEAH — Much prized by sorcerers and voodooists who use it in magical rites and rituals.

To remove any evil spell, have the bewitched one wear a piece of burdock root in a bag around the neck. As you place the necklace on the person, anoint the crown of the head with the Obeah Oil and have the jinxed one count from 50 to 1 backwards. As the jinxed one is counting backwards, you count from 1 to 50 in the usual order. This spell should banish any curse, and its effectiveness should last for fifty days, after which it can be repeated if necessary.

OLIBANUM — Same as Frankincense Oil. A holy oil, believed to be a powerful protection against black magic.

Ōō free one from possession by satanic forces, apply the oil to the forehead, throat, and chest while repeating Psalm 145.

Use it to dress candles and burn them in the home to keep evil from the premises.

ORANGE — Highly magnetic oil which attracts men when used as a perfume by women.

It is added to incense and burned in voodoo services to bring harmony and power to the room.

ORANGE BLOSSOM — This scent is said to put one in a marrying mood, and brings proposals from reluctant lovers.

All brides should wear this on the wedding day to insure a long and happy marriage.

ORCHID — One of the most guarded secrets of occult work is the way toward total concentration on the problem on which one is at work. Since one's entire mind powers must be marshalled to bring results, this oil is used to aid one's ability to properly focus their attention. It is applied to the temples during prayers of meditation.

Others use it as a perfume to aid the memory and to help focus their thoughts on the job or problem at hand.

ORIENTAL — From the mysterious East comes a distinctive fragrance dedicated to the graceful living few of us in the western world have practiced.

Apply to the temples and wrists as you concentrate on

Robert Southwell's verse whose message reminds us that serenity and peace of mind come from within, not from outside influence or other people:

> My conscience is my crown,
> Contented thoughts my rest.
> My heart is happy in itself,
> My bliss is in my breast.

OUIJA — Use when you wish to receive telepathic messages from someone who is a distance away from you.

Before you apply the oil to the fingertips, find a quiet secluded area away from traffic noises, television or radio turned off, phone unplugged, door closed so that there are no interruptions from visitors.

Sit in a comfortable chair, or lie down on the bed. Anoint the fingertips and place the hands together in a praying hands position. Close the eyes and concentrate only on seeing a glowing full moon on a distant horizon. Soon after this scene is visualized, muted vocal sounds will transmit into the mind, clues, answers, or helpful input bearing on a problem or troublesome situation which has been a burden.

To use with the Ouija Board, apply to the fingertips so that the planchette will move more rapidly and, consequently, produce prompter results.

OWE ME — Use this when waiting for money which is overdue.

If the payment is expected by mail, rub the oil around the edges of the post box or door slot. Should the debtor be available in person, dab some of the oil on the back of their wrists. While applying it, meditate on this chant:

> Bring back that which is mine own,
> Not yours, but mine alone.
> Send only what is due to me,
> And blessed with more you will be.

P

PARADISE — Whatever your vision of true bliss may be, bring it into closer focus when you use this heavenly scent.

Apply to the ear lobes, forehead, and ankles — so that all that you hear or think will be blessed, and your steps will be guided on the path toward your own personal seventh heaven.

PARTING — While separation can be painful occasions, the resulting melancholy can be eased by this meditation. Repeat as often as necessary, until the ache is bearable or has faded away, this short verse by Frances R. Havergal, 19th Century English poet and hymn composer:

> Just to let thy Father do
> What He will;
> Just to know that He is true,
> And be still;
> Just to trust Him, that is all!
> Then the day will surely be
> Peaceful, whatso'er befall,
> Bright and blessed, calm and free.

PASSION — One of the most potent of the love oils — it is said to work when others have been unsuccessful. The coldest of lovers often turns into the most amorous suitor when this is applied to the arms and legs.

To heighten one's own passions, add to the bath water.

PASSION FLOWER — An exciting fragrance which heightens one's amorous feelings and should be used sparingly. A drop behind each knee and on the elbows should be quite adequate to arouse one's passions to an exciting, but not wanton, level.

PATCHOULI — An oil of many attributes. It is regarded as an aphrodisiac with magical powers.

It is used to bring peace to the home, settle arguments, and calm strife. When rubbed on another person, it generally calms their anger and quiets their wrath.

Anoint the doorknob of the home or an apartment to cause a troublemaker to depart or move away peacefully.

PAY ME — Those slow payers need a reminder urging them to keep current with payments due to others. Should some of your receivables be lagging behind their due dates, there is a method which can often bring fast results.

Soak a penny in this potent oil for twenty-four hours. Then take it and place it in the center of a large piece of parchment paper or stationery. Around all the edges of the talisman scribe with dip pen in Dragon's Blood Ink the following short verse:

Repay your debts without delays.

Your reward will be happy days.

Send it to the debtor and expect payments to arrive before a week has passed. Whether you sign the message sent is a personal decision.

The recipient will be alerted to all his or her responsibilities and perhaps will be inclined to honor all the obligations due to others.

PEACE — Apply to your person or sprinkle about the home to bring quiet and tranquility into your life.

Make yourself a "serenity charm" by drawing on a square of parchment paper a triangle and, within it, a cross. Use Dove's Blood Ink and write your name on the outside of the triangle three times, once on each side. Anoint each corner of the talisman with Peace Oil daily for continued calm in life and harmony in the home.

PEACEFUL HOME — Insure a serene and tranquil domestic life by using the Peaceful Home Incense weekly to clear the premises of all baneful vibrations.

To enhance the calm atmosphere of the premises, apply a drop of oil to one or several small cotton balls and place them at strategic points so that they waft their soothing odor over the entire home.

PENNYROYAL — Anoint the four corners of a Seal of Fortune from the Sixth & Seventh Books of Moses and on the back of the seal write the amount of money you need for your specific goal. Or, if applicable, scribe the names of the person you need to cooperate with you on a planned financial transaction.

Carry the charm, reanointing it every third day to keep the magic working.

The objective should be fulfilled before the second week has passed.

PEONY — A lucky perfume for all those who need customers, success in business, or good fortune in all one's endeavors.

The store will prosper indeed if near the cash register or drawer is kept a Schemhamphoras No. 1 Seal from the Sixth and Seventh Books of Moses and it is dressed with this oil each morning before the doors are opened to customers.

PEPPERMINT — Add spice to your life and pep to your body with this exciting oil. Get things changing and moving when you add a few drops to your floor wash, in the bath, or mixed with an incense you are using.

To use the oil as a hexing agent, it is rubbed on candles when one's intention is to bring harm and havoc to an enemy. In Dragon's Blood Ink, write the foe's name on parchment and place the paper beneath a black candle. After the candle is dressed with the oil, light it and let it burn until consumed.

It can also be sprinkled on a foe's clothes, automobile,

or doorsteps tó cause him to encounter damaging and demoralizing situations.

PIKAKI — Promotes the good things in life: comfort, good health, friendships. Anoint the throat, palms, and ankles daily.

PINE — A cleansing, purifying scent used in the bath to wash away past mistakes and sins, permitting one to start afresh without wasting one's energies on useless recriminations.

PINEAPPLE — To draw back a lover who has gone, anoint a candle with the oil and place under the candle this request which you have written in Dove's Blood Ink on parchment paper: "Let this light see (insert name of the one you wish to attract) and bring him (or her) to me and bind him (or her) to me forever." Burn the candle each day for ten minutes at sunset until your loved one has returned. If your object is a male, use an orange candle. If female, use pink or red candle.

PISCES (February 20 to March 20) — The House of Invention and Justice. Jupiter is ruling planet. Friday is your lucky day. Lucky numbers are 1 and 2. While Pisces people are kind, moral, capable, methodical, and logical, they often lack the ability to discern dishonesty and untrustworthiness in others. Wear this special scent to help you interpret the intentions of those around you. Those born under this sign are often gifted with clairvoyant abilities, so develop them by wearing this when you attempt to contact the spirits, read the minds of others, or send telepathic messages.

PLANETARY OILS — Each sign of the zodiac is ruled by a planet, and the qualities of the ruling planet seem to influence the personality of those born under that particular ruler. Check below to find the ruling planet for your birthdate, and find that special oil listed under the specific planet's name. Planetary oils can be used by everybody — not just those whose birth corresponds in the table given below — for the attributes of the various planets are desired or needed by all people from time to time.

If you were born between:	See:
January 21 and February 19	Uranus
February 20 and March 20	Jupiter
March 21 and April 20	Mars
April 21 and May 22	Venus
May 23 and June 21	Mercury
June 22 and July 22	Moon
July 23 and August 22	Sun
August 23 and September 22	Mercury
September 23 and October 22	Venus
October 23 and November 21	Mars
November 22 and December 22	Jupiter
December 23 and January 20	Saturn

PLUMERIA — This beautiful fragrant red jasmine of the West Indies is most suitable to wear as a perfume on any occasion, but especially when it is important that others should notice you and listen to what you have to say.

Be prepared with facts and figures on a proposal you may want to advance, and people will consider seriously — and usually favorably — your ideas and plans.

PLUTO — The invisible sovereign of the underworld inspired this fragrance. Pluto was the god of agricultural wealth, and from his abode in the center of the earth influenced crops and cultivation.

Farmers may wish to sprinkle a few drops in the rows where seeds are being planted to encourage an abundant crop.

In classical mythology Pluto was also the god of the dead.

One may wish to enlist his protection of the souls of your departed ones. Sprinkle the grave and pray this short petition:

Peace be with you, my departed friend.
Though apart forever we are not.
Love we shared and share forever,
Rest in peace 'till we meet again.

POPPY — Anoint your money with this oil so that it may spawn as prolifically as the poppy plant's seeds and multiply as quickly.

POTPOURRI — A mixture of scents formulated for use as a daily perfume, or for some specific objectives.

To have your written request for assistance received favorably, place a drop of the oil on the envelope beneath the spot where the stamp will be placed.

For a personal desire, anoint a white candle — from the center downward — with the oil. Write your wish or request in Dove's Blood Ink on parchment and place it beneath the candle. Repeat this affirmation three times as you ignite the flame:

Light my path that I may walk in the direction
which will result in the fulfillment of my requirement.

POWER — To overcome another's power over you, use five drops in the bath each day. As you soak, repeat this chant several times:

I have the power, I have the will,
My own destiny I must fulfill.
No other man can subdue me
God alone can undo me.

This same little chant helps to increase one's own powers whenever it is used. Repeat it often and anoint the crown of the head with the oil upon arising each morning.

To conquer an enemy who is working against you, make a rough image of the human body on heavy cardboard or wood, or use one of the authentic wooden fetishes which are occasionally available from occult stores or African gift shops. Take nine new nails and soak them for nine full days in the Power Oil. Then, for nine days, one nail at a time, drive a nail into the "doll" and chant:

> Leave my life, let me be,
> Go in peace, set me free.

All influence that person has had over you will have been destroyed by the time the nine nails are in place in the effigy.

PRAYER — In times of stress, a simple ritual can relieve the tension, soothe the nerves, and bring one's emotions under control so that the petition can be offered in a serene confident manner.

Begin your prayer with a dab of the oil on the forehead and this affirmation:

> Father, I seek patience, clarity of mind,
> freedom from anxiety, a restful spirit, and
> complete faith in Thy loving kindness.

Be still and silent for a few moments and then continue with your specific supplication.

PRIMROSE — This scent is believed to draw the truth from any liar. If one is suspected, place a drop of the oil on their clothes, in their shoes, or rub directly onto their body and it will cause them to make a clean breast of whatever they have been false about.

PROMOTION — Advance your career by applying yourself energetically to your job. Be prompt, neat, clean and enthusiastic.

Adopt the following poem from the pen of Henry van Dyke as a daily reading just before going to work:

> Let me but do my work from day to day,
> In field or forest, at the desk or loom,
> In roaring market place or tranquil room.
> Let me but find it in my heart to say,

When vagrant wishes beckon me astray,
"This is my work; my blessing, not my doom;
Of all who live, I am the one by whom
This work can best be done in the right way."
Then shall I see it not too great, nor small,
To suit my spirit and to prove my powers;
Then shall I cheerful greet the laboring hours,
And cheerful turn, when the long shadows fall
At eventide, to play and love and rest,
Because I know for me my work is best.

Apply the oil to the wrists after the reading and go to your job, knowing that your efforts will be appreciated and rewarded with an opportunity to go forward and upward in your chosen profession.

PROSPERITY — Very similar to Wealthy Way Oil. It attracts and draws luck and success in business deals, and in gambling. Anoint your lucky charms with it, wear it as a perfume when discussing financial matters, and rub it on the wrists before shuffling the cards or throwing the dice.

Wear it to work when in search of a raise in pay.

PROTECTION — Wear on the neck and ankles as a guard against jinxes, curses, and the Evil Eye.

A truly invincible talisman is formed by carrying a cross — any kind will do, either plain or the crucifix form with Jesus on the the cross — in a red flannel bag which is anointed every Sunday with the Protection Oil. While anointing the bag, repeat The Lord's Prayer.

PROTECTION FROM ENVY — "Envy is the most corroding of the vices, and also the greatest power in the land," according to James M. Barrie, English novelist and playwright. No pleasure nor contentment can grow and thrive until envy is expelled from a relationship.

Get a white jumbo or seven-day candle and anoint it

from the base upward with the oil. Beneath the candle place a square of parchment on which you have copied in Dove's Blood Ink Verses 1 through 4 of Psalm 140:

> Deliver me, O Lord, from the evil man.
> Preserve me from the violent man,
> which imagine mischiefs in their heart,
> continually are they gathered together for war.
> They have sharpened their tongues like a ser-
> pent;
> adder's poison is under their lips. Selah.
> Keep me, O Lord, from the hands of the
> wicked;
> preserve me from the violent man,
> who have proposed to overthrow my goings.

Serenity and peace of mind will come into your heart before a week has passed.

PROTECTION FROM HARM — After the morning bath, surround yourself with the mantle of faith which provides security from all injury, violence, or malicious mischief.

Apply a dab of the oil to the soles of the feet, wrists, and forehead as you pray St. Patrick's protection prayer:

> I bind to myself today
> God's power to guide me,
> God's might to uphold me,
> God's wisdom to teach me,
> God's ear to hear me,
> God's eye to watch over me,
> God's word to give me speech,
> God's hand to guard me,
> God's way to lie before me,
> God's shield to protect me
> against the snares of demons,
> against the seduction of vices,
> against the lusts of nature,
> against those who wish me ill.
> Christ, protect me today.

PSYCHIC — Expand one's extrasensory perceptions and telepathic powers with this concentrated essence.

Intensify the sixth sense with an application of the oil on the palms, at the temples, and on the soles of the feet. Then lie down, or sit comfortably in a lounge chair, so that the body can totally relax. Close the eyes, putting all mundane thoughts out of the mind. Chant this rhyme softly till a sign or vision comes into being:

There is a world beyond my ken.
Bring it forth into view.
Show to me that I have not seen,
And tell me things I never knew.

"Q" — No one seems to know where the "Q" comes from or what its full name is — today it is always just Q Oil or Oil of Q. It is worn as a perfume when one desires to arouse sensuous thoughts or sexual desires in another. Very enticing, so use cautiously.

QUEEN OF SHEBA — An alluring fragrance which entices friends, bewitches lovers, and causes complete strangers to favor the wearer.

To bring a proposal of marriage from a reluctant suitor, draw on a square of parchment with Dove's Blood Ink a ring — artistic ability does not matter, just a simple double circle will do. In the center of the ring write your name, and outside the ring write the loved one's name. Place this talisman in a red flannel bag and place it beneath the pillow or mattress on which you sleep, anointing it weekly with the oil, as you chant,

Lover, lover, come to me. Be by my side forevermore.
Lover, lover, marry me, For you I do adore.

QUEEN OF TIBET — Exotic, tantalizing, spellbinding! A producer of passion. This very special oil is used by those who want the most, need the most, and expect the most of everything out of life.

QUICK MONEY — Use only when the need is urgent and your usual sources are not available.

Take all the paper money in your possession and anoint the two upper corners of each bill. As you do this, pray sincerely Verses 6 through 9 of Psalm 122:

Pray for the peace of Jerusalem:
they shall prosper that love thee.
Peace be within thy wall,
and prosperity within thy palaces.
For my brethren and companions' sakes,
I will now say, Peace be within thee.
Because of the house of the Lord our God,
I will seek thy good.

Replace the bills into the pocket or wallet with confidence that unexpected riches will come to you before the anointed money is exhausted.

QUICK MONEY DRAWING — Used to draw cash, treasures, and other good fortune, thereby gaining financial security.

Sprinkle across the doorway to the home or place of business, and apply to the windowsills and doorknobs. As you do this, chant at each point this simple petition:

May the blessings be many,
And the troubles be few.
May there be gold in the pocket,
And all wishes soon come true.

R

RACE TRACK — Increase your chances of picking the winners by anointing the edges of all tickets, the program, and your fingertips while making your selections.

RADIANT HEALTH — Try this to regain or maintain one's natural state of being sound in body, mind and spirit.

Anoint the afflicted one at the point of pain or on the affected area, if applicable. Should the purpose be for general healing or for maintaining one's well-being, place a drop of the oil at wrists, ankles, and back of the neck.

A suitable affirmation to accompany the ritual can be one's own personal preference, or Psalm 23:

> The Lord is my shepherd, I shall not want.
> He maketh me to lie down in green pastures.
> He leadeth me beside the still waters.
> He restoreth my soul.
> He leadest me in the paths of righteousness
>   for his name's sake.
> Yea, though I walk through the valley of the
>   shadow of death, I will fear no evil,
> for thou art with me.
> Thy rod and thy staff, they comfort me.
> Thou preparest a table before me in the presence of mine enemies;
> Thou anointest my head with oil;
> My cup runneth over.
> Surely goodness and mercy shall follow me
> all the days of my life:
> and I will dwell in the house of the Lord forever.

RED FAST LUCK — For success in any business transaction, use this fast action lucky oil.

Sprinkle the entrances to one's place of business each

morning as the doors are opened. Within the establishment, use a few drops in those areas where merchandise is not moving as well as it should be.

To draw money to you personally, anoint the fingertips before going out to sell merchandise or to collect money owed to you.

RED ROSE — One of the most effective love oils to aid one in drawing affection, tenderness, and passion when nothing else has made a difference.

After the bath chant as you apply drops of oil to the backs of the hands, neckline, and to the heels of the feet:

> Red, red rose, flower of the heart,
> Surround my love and bind it fast.
> Keep it strong so that we may never part,
> Make it true and constant, let it last.

REMOVING — Replace obstacles with opportunities by a life of submission to God and obedience to His commandments. As a help toward this objective, copy Verses 7 through 10 of Psalm 34 onto a piece of parchment:

> The poor man cried, and the Lord heard him,
> and saved him out of all his troubles,
> The angel of the Lord encampeth round about
>   them
> that fear him, and delivereth them.
> O taste and see that the Lord is good;
> Blessed is the man that trusteth in him.
> O fear the Lord, ye his saints;
> for there is no want to them that fear him.
> The young lions do lack, and suffer hunger;
> but they that seek the Lord shall not want any
>   good thing.

Read the verses daily and anoint the corners of the paper with the oil. Wrap the talisman in a clean white handkerchief and repeat the ritual each day until the barriers in your path toward success have been removed.

REPELLING — If you wish to keep visitors from the home, sprinkle this across the outside of the entrances. Chant as you apply it so that unwanted visitors will be repulsed:

> Go away, stay away,
> You are not welcome here,
> Retrace your steps, I say,
> Just leave and disappear.

Repeat this weekly to insure that you will not be disturbed.

RETURN TO ME — Draw back an estranged friend or loved one with an apple, red cord or string, sugar, and a white square of cloth. A handkerchief is a good choice.

Purchase a red apple and split it in half. With a small sharp knife, remove the core from both halves.

With Dove's Blood Ink write the name of the one you wish to return on a small square of parchment paper. Sprinkle over the name a small amount of sugar. Then roll or fold the paper into as small a packet as possible, and tie it tightly with the string.

Place the charm in the hollowed out center of the apple, and put the other half back in its original position. Wrap the cloth or handkerchief tightly around the charm, tying it securely with cord so that it remains firmly in place.

Bury the charm close to your home, and mark the spot so that you can anoint it with a few drops of oil each day until you and your beloved are together again.

REVENGE — Place beneath a black candle a square of parchment on which you have scribed in Dragon's Blood Ink the name of the one you desire to come to harm. Anoint the candle with oil — from center to base — and sprinkle salt around the candle holder. Light the candle and allow it to burn until consumed. The object of the ritual should not bother you again, as he or she will be besieged by the same kind of devilment which was put upon you.

REVERSE EVIL — Should a curse stand between you and your objectives, send it back to the one who placed the hex in your path. Clear the premises by burning some of the Reversible Incense, and rub the oil on the outside doorknobs at all entrances.

As you do the anointing, pray this short prayer by Digby M. Dolbern, 19th century English poet:

> From falsehood and error,
> From darkness and terror,
> From all that is evil,
> From the power of the devil,
> From the fire and the doom,
> From the judgment to come,
> Sweet Jesus, deliver
> Thy servants forever.

REVERSIBLE — This is to be used when complete chaos seems to have surrounded you and there appears to be no solution to the problems with which you are faced. Sprinkle the oil in the home, use in the bath, and on the body. Repeat this passage from Psalm 37:

> Lord, do not punish me in your anger,
> do not chastise me in your wrath.
> For your arrows have pierced me deep,
> Heavy upon me is your hand.
> There is no health in my body because of your
>   anger,
> no soundness in my bones because of my sin.
> For my iniquities have risen over my head,
> like an immense burden, they weigh me down.

Do this daily until you have broken the negative forces which have enveloped you and the powers of light have been given their chance to enter your sphere and spread their healing, life-giving rays.

ROAD OPENER — Opportunity may not knock at your door unless you keep the pathway to it clean and inviting. This applies to the place where one lives as well as the personal body.

If visitors to the home are welcome, apply a few drops to the doorknob.

This same fragrance is used as a perfume on the body when you go to find a job so that you will be received favorably by the interviewer.

ROSE — A gentle love oil, used as a perfume by all to attract affection and love.

To bring peace to the home or the place where you work, get about two tablespoonsful of rose buds or petals. If you have fresh roses in your yard, use those, or purchase dried packets from an occult supply house or any good gift shop. Place the roses in a small container and pour over them a bottle of Rose Oil. Leave the dish undisturbed for three full days, and on the fourth day sprinkle the rose petals around the premises as you recite the 23rd Psalm. Peace will surely follow.

ROSE ALTAR — An uplifting scent which is used to draw positive and promising conditions into your life. Apply to the appropriate candle — white for spiritual objectives, pink or red for love and attraction, green for improving financial matters. Light and burn until the candle is consumed.

ROSE GERANIUM — A blessing and protection oil used to anoint altars, homes, and any personal possessions.

Add to the scrub water to protect the home from adverse conditions and to reverse misfortune. It is believed to protect the premises from malicious mischief.

Wear it as a perfume to turn back vicious gossip toward the one who started the rumor.

ROSE OF CRUCIFIXION — Worn to dispel fear and protect from all crossed conditions.

Your Seal of Long Life talisman, which protects from misfortune and misery, and assures one of a lengthy life, should be anointed with this oil every seven days.

ROSE OF JERICHO — Resurrect your faith, confidence, and zest for living by using this as your daily perfume. Apply the energizing fragrance to the temples each morning after your cleansing bath or shower, and pray this small devotion:

Thank you, God, for the blessings I will receive this day. Increase my faith in goodness and mercy so that, as I give these gifts to others, they may be returned to me in kind.

ROSEMARY — One of the most ancient English herbs, rosemary was kept in the home during the Christmas season as a token of hospitality to elves and other friendly spirits. In today's occult world, the oil is regarded as one of the most powerful weapons against Black Magic, hatred, and evil of all kinds. It is worn on the temples, wrists, and ankles.

Rosemary Oil is highly respected as a healing oil, used to ease the pains of both headache and heartsickness.

To insure a good night's sleep, boil two cups of water to which you have added one-fourth cup of War Water and nine drops of the oil. Let cool and place the container under the bed before retiring.

RUE — Can be worn as a perfume to protect one from the hexes set out by others toward us.

Add a few drops of the oil to Protection Incense and burn so that the evil spirits go up in the smoke. At the same time the smoke draws malevolent forces out of the body so that at the same time the dynamic and radiant powers of good can enter to vitalized and illuminate our life.

The Rue Oil has very special attributes as an antidote to madness, and is believed to be very healing to those who are mentally or emotionally disturbed. Add to the bath water to soothe and calm.

RUN DEVIL RUN — Satan simply cannot abide this scent and will not tarry in the vicinity where it is used.

Sprinkle it outside all doorways and on the windowsills so that no evil spirits can gain entry to the home. Renew once a week, preferably every Saturday.

S

SABBAT — A ritual oil for the celebrations held by witches at each full moon observance, plus eight other annual celebrations.

Candlemas, the fire festival .... February 2

Spring Equinox, first day of spring .... March 21

Ruemas, fertility celebration .... May 1

Beltane, first day of summer .... June 21

Lammas, prosperity celebration .... August 1

Autumn Equinox, thanksgiving rite .... September 21

Hallowman (Halloween), honoring souls of the dead and return of the other world spirits .... October 31

Yule, winter solstice .... December 21

Sprinkle the oil to designate the perimeters of the magic circle before the rites begin.

SACRED — This is formulated for use in anointing the candles and utensils in all Wicca rituals or religious ceremonies.

A proper invocation could be similar to this example:

I call upon Diana,
goddess of the moon, light, mountains, and woods,
bless these utensils
and the ceremony in which they are utilized.
Blessed be.

SAFFRON — Used by mediums, clairvoyants, and all those who wish to foresee the future. Rub on the forehead before consulting the crystal ball, laying the cards, or throwing the runes.

SAGITTARIUS (November 22 to December 22) — The House of Speculation and Travel. Jupiter is ruling planet. Lucky day is Thursday. Lucky numbers are 1 and 6. One of the most fortunate of all signs, Sagittariuses are strong, vigorous, fearless, good friends, confident, faithful, moral, and blessed with many other good qualities. Their most damaging quality can be that they are often abrupt and impatient with others who are not so enterprising or bright as themselves. So conserve your time and energy, and preserve your friendships with others by using this specially blended scent which will subtly soothe your emotions so that you do not have to speak sharply to others — and make your motto, "Easy does it."

ST. ALEX — An early Christian martyr of whom little is known was the inspiration for the fragrance which reputedly protects one from malicious mischief and harm by adversaries.

Apply to the inside of the elbows and backs of the knees each morning after the bath. As you do this, pray sincerely this prayer by Alcuin, 8th Century scholar, educator, and theologian:

Eternal light, shine into our hearts.
Eternal goodness, deliver us from all evil.
Eternal power, grant us strength.
Eternal wisdom, break the bond of our ignorance.
Eternal pity, have mercy on us.
May we seek you with all our heart, mind,
soul, and strength,
and come to share your holy presence forever.
Amen.

ST. ANTHONY — For a truly peaceful, blessed life, place in your home an image of St. Anthony (a prayer card, picture on the wall, or a statue are all equally effective). Each day, upon arising, anoint the saint's likeness and your own palms and wrists. Stand or kneel before the image and pray sincerely and with faith:

> Take from my heart all anger, bitterness, ugliness, and rebellion. Replace it with hope and patience and confidence. Bring success to my endeavors this day for I sorely need thy help in all that I attempt. I thank thee that thou hast heard me in this prayer.

ST. BARBARA — This 3rd Century Christian was the daughter of Dioscorus, an idolater, who had a white marble bath made for Barbara's use. When she first entered it, she drew a cross with her finger, and the mark remained even though her father tried to have it obliterated. Hundreds of others using the bath kissed the cross and were healed of their infirmities or diseases.

Should you be in need of a healing, anoint the forehead and temples with this fragrance and pray daily until the condition is improved:

> Look down from heaven, I pray, with eyes of mercy. Strengthen this ailing body, comfort this worried mind, and bring confidence to a wavering spirit. With thy help, perfect health will be restored to this weak and fragile one.
> Amen.

ST. CHRISTOPHER — Dedicated to the most popular of saints, this formula is a protective oil which, as promised in an ancient rhyme, will keep you safe throughout the day.

Each morning, apply to the back of the knees and inside of the elbows. Stand before a likeness of the saint, and chant three times this simple verse:

> If thou the face of Christopher
> on any morn shall see,
> Through the day from sudden death
> thou shalt preserved be.

ST. CLARE — See Santa Clara

ST. EXPEDITUS — When you need quick action on an urgent problem, put your faith in the ultimate goodness of God and use this legendary oil.

One of the favorite ways to use the oil is to write your problem on a piece of parchment, anoint the paper at each corner with oil, and burn the paper. Repeat this procedure daily for seven days and your situation should be bettered.

ST. IGNATIUS — Countless wonders have been credited to the relics of this 16th Century saint. His clothing cured the plague. A relic, cast into the sea, calmed the waves and stilled the wind. His picture scared away devils. Just the writing of his name on a piece of paper brought untold healings.

Write your particular request on parchment, place it in an envelope, and seal the talisman by applying the oil to the envelope flap.

ST. JOSEPH — Use for a good life with confidence in heavenly protection and pray daily:

This day I pray thee to protect those I love, and those who love me. Grant us whatever we need that is good for us. Teach us to be content, to do our work gladly. Bring joy and satisfaction to all our contacts, and bestow upon us the grace of thy great and tender love. Help us to do thy will in gratitude for all thy gifts.

ST. JUDE — The "saint of the impossible" has been utilized by employing his name for this psychic oil which is reserved for specially severe cases where all else has failed. Apply to an image of St. Jude and wear or carry it in the pocket. Pray and repeat Psalm 23 daily.

ST. MARTHA — Sister of Mary and Lazarus, Martha was hostess to Jesus when he visited at Bethany. The practical one, Martha is credited with being able to supply one with the necessities of life. When you are in need, write your request on parchment paper. As you pray this short petition, anoint the edges of the talisman with the oil:

> St. Martha, I come for thy aid and protection.
> Comfort me in all my difficulties,
> and through the great favors thou didst enjoy
> when the Saviour was lodged in thy house,
> intercede for my family that we may be provid-
>   ed with our necessities.
> I ask thee, Blessed Martha,
> to obtain for us the grace to overcome
> all obstacles which confront us.

ST. MARTIN CABALLERO — For those who seek faith, forgiveness, or release from guilt for past sins of omission or commission, use this essence along with the following petition to bring serenity and confidence in one's own inner goodness.

Copy the prayer onto a sheet of parchment paper and then roll the paper into a cylinder with the writing on the inner side. Tie the talisman with white string or ribbon so that it is secure. Each day apply a drop of oil to the edge of the paper, undo the fastener, unroll the paper, and pray sincerely:

> Blessed Saint, you were born under pagan
>   ways
> but since your childhood you were chosen
> to be a Prince of the Church and,
> as Bishop of Tours, many souls were re-
>   deemed
> and liberated from the satanic forces
> through your prayers, austerities, and bless-
>   ings.
> I humbly beg for your intercession before our

Lord Jesus Christ because we want to be worthy
of the grace and mercy of the Holy Spirit
that leads us from darkness to light
into the eternal kingdom, forever and ever.
Amen.

ST. MARTIN DE PORRES — Do you find it hard to accept people
for what they are rather than by first impressions based on
physical features and quality of their clothing?

If you hesitate before responding to the question, you
will find your life enriched by realizing that the color of one's
hair, eyes, or skin has little or nothing to do with the innate
goodness or evil within each of us.

St. Martin was the son of a Spanish knight and a black
feed slave. He learned how to cure diseases, and gave himself to God as a Dominican brother. His charity was so extended that he kept a home for "wandering cats and dogs",
and offered himself for sale when his community needed
money!

The oil dedicated to him can bring dignity and respect to
all who believe that goodness is rewarded and evil is pun-
ished, no matter the color of one's skin or the balance in the
bank account.

Pray daily as the wrists and ankles are anointed with the
scent, Verse 24 of Psalm 31:

Be of good courage,
and He shall strengthen your heart,
all ye that hope in the Lord.

ST. MARY MAGDALENE — While her origins remain shrouded in
mystery, it seems most probable that Mary Magdalene was
the sinner about which Jesus says in Luke 7, Verses 47, 48,
and 50:

"Her sins, which are many, are forgiven; for
she loved much: but to whom little is forgiv-

en, the same loveth little...Thy sins are forgiv-
en...Thy faith hath saved thee, go in peace."

Should you be in need of pardon for wrongs you may
now regret, this oil can be used with a short prayer along with
a drop of oil onto the back of the neck:

Oh, Lord, your tender mercies,
your loving kindness,
and pardon of our iniquities,
is sorely needed. Bless me, Father.

ST. MICHAEL — Alleged to bring great powers to those who apply
it to their hands before doing occult work. Keep some open in
the room wherever psychic skill is employed.

To conquer the obstacles in one's path, secure an image
of St. Michael (a statue, a picture or prayer card, or a paper
seal picturing the crossed swords which is called the Shield
of St. Michael). Anoint your talisman daily with the oil, and
pray this prayer faithfully:

Thy help is my salvation, and I ask for assistance in
guarding me from all danger, delivering me from all evil of
body and soul. Free my enemies from the bondage of hatred,
let not anger burn in their hearts, and instill in them the peace
and love and forgiveness toward me which I bear toward
them. Let me by my example prove my sincerity in my efforts
to turn away from all rage and wrath, inviting in its place tranquility and serenity.

ST. PETER — For help with any problem, secure a Master Key Seal
which is a design associated with, but not taken from, the
Sixth and Seventh Books of Moses. On the back of the seal,
write out your problem briefly. Anoint each corner of the seal
with this oil, then fold the paper in half, then in half again, and
place it inside a red flannel bag which you will then carry on
your person at all times until your dilemma is cleared up.
Each morning and evening anoint the bag with three drops of
the St. Peter Oil.

SAN CIPRIANO — To gain spiritual help, wear on the ear lobes and on the wrists.

A highly magnetic attracting oil, it is worn to bring back wandering husbands, wives, or lovers.

Wear to court for help with legal problems.

SAN JACOBS — A specially blended oil for use on backs of the hands and ears to attract money, wealth, and power.

SAN LAZARO (St. Lazarus) — The brother of Mary and Martha, raised from the dead after four days by Jesus, represents the miracle of rebirth which can happen to all of us at any time it is needed.

When depressed, dispirited, or despondent (a living death of the spirit) — feeling that nothing is right and everything is wrong — anoint the feet, hands, and ears while you meditate on this simple prayer:

> God, thank you for these feet — that hurt, and ache from time to time. Bless them for I will never have others.
>
> And thank you for these hands — stiff, awkward, worn as they are.
>
> My eyes are dim, and my ears miss a nuance at times — but I am not blind nor deaf.
>
> Help me, God, to always dwell not on what I've lost nor never had, but with that which I am still blessed. Amen.

SAN RAFAEL — Dedicated to healing maladies of the spirit and of the body, this can be applied to the ill person's forehead, neckline, and soles of the feet along with a prayer for an improvement of health:

> Holy Father, bless me now, I pray.
> Strengthen me this day
> That I may go about my daily task,

With humility and love I do ask.
Thank you for all blessings,
And lead me onward to love and Thee.

SAN RAMON — To bring new customers, mix nine drops with a teaspoon of new salt and sprinkle it across the doorway or entrance to your place of business so that all who pass may pause and enter your establishment. Do this weekly, or more often if necessary.

SANCTUARY — Any place can become one's private serene retreat with the proper attitude and a simple meditation.

It is helpful if you can play a relaxing, soothing tape or recording — spring sounds, babbling brook, soft music — whatever your personal preference may be.

Lie down on a comfortable bed or lounge, dressed comfortably. Soothe the temples with the oil, close the eyes, and use this simple prayer:

Dear God, stay by my side,
Gaze upon me; Come with me everywhere
So that I am not alone.
Come from heaven into my heart.

SANDALWOOD — Oil from the sacred sandalwood tree is used in many perfumes and medicines. A powerful healing oil, especially good for bruised areas.

The use of this helps develop one's clairvoyant powers. Try it by applying to the temples before a seance, or to the hands before asking a question of the Ouija Board. For those who are attempting clear seeing (being able to see people, objects, or events at a long distance away), apply to the upper eye lids before concentrating.

SANTA CLARA (St. Clare) — Dedicated to this friend of St. Francis of Assisi, and founder of the religious order of nuns now called the "Poor Clares", this scent is a protective one —

shielding the wearer from violence of all kinds.

When afraid, feeling threatened, or troubled by nebulous apprehension, pray this small prayer to regain confidence and serenity:

Thou knowest, Lord, my fear,
cast it from me and give me strength.
Take away my trembling and anxiety,
And grant me faith in the knowledge
that I am safe within Thy shield of love.

SASSAFRAS — Formulated to bring a favorable decision from the court when it is sprinkled on a handkerchief and taken to the courtroom. Use it in all sessions with one's lawyer before the trial, and in any legal negotiations.

To be free of another's power over you, prepare seven pieces of parchment by writing on each of them with Dragon's Blood Ink this simple phrase:

I break your power (name of controller);
I destroy your force (name of controller);
I deny your control over me (name of controller)

Each evening, for seven consecutive days, moisten one of the papers thoroughly in the Sassafras Oil and then tear it into three pieces. Mix the paper with Damnation Incense and burn it until it is consumed. Each day the power of the one who has been manipulating you will be less and less, and by the end of the week all control will have vanished.

SATAN BE GONE — This can be used for uncrossing when one suspects that Satan's forces have entered either the home or the person. Applied daily to the temples it cleanses the mind and body, and applied to outside doorknobs of the home keeps the premises safe from intrusion by evil.

For those who fear ghosts, evil spirits, or apparitions of any kind a potent protective talisman can be made by writing with Dove's Blood Ink on pure parchment paper the 18th, 19th, and 20th verses of Psalm 145, as given here:

The Lord is nigh unto all them that call upon him,
to all that call upon him in truth.
He will fulfil the desire of them that fear him,
he also will hear their cry, and will save them.
The Lord preserveth all them that love him,
but all the wicked will he destroy.

Place this talisman in a red flannel or leather case and carry it on the person, anointing it each morning with the Satan Be Gone Oil. Be sure that divine protection will follow you wherever you go.

SATURN — One of the planetary oils, and one of many uses. To gain success in business ventures, to impose your will upon others, or to protect yourself and your possessions, use on your own body.

To strengthen one's capacity to perform jobs or carry out one's duties and responsibilities, make a Table of Saturn on parchment. This is a square of 3, using numbers 1 to 9. Each column totals 15, and the total of all is 45. Place numbers 4, 9, 2 in the top row. Numbers 3, 5, 7 in the middle row, and 8, 1, 6 in the bottom row. Draw a square around the numbers, then a line between the numbers vertically and horizontally, resulting in a square of the nine numbers, with each in a separate square. Anoint this talisman with the Saturn Oil once a week and carry it with you at all times.

To cause a foe to be possessed by demons, secure a design called the Sixth Pentacle of Saturn, which is illustrated in the book titled, "The Greater Key of Solomon." Some occult supply houses offer this talisman for sale, or you can trace it yourself from the book if you prefer. Hold the talisman in one hand as you rub the Saturn Oil along its outer edges and pronounce the enemy's name, repeating "Set thou a wicked one to be ruler over him and let Satan stand at his right hand." The Pentacle should then be buried or burned at once.

SATYR — A satyr is not a devil as many erroneously believe, but is a Greek mythological god of the forests or woods. He is usually represented as part man and part goat with horns on the head, a hairy body, and the feet and tail of a goat.

The oil bearing this creature's name is believed to represent the satyr's qualities of refinement and perpetual youth. Use it as a daily perfume when you wish to accentuate these qualities in yourself.

SCORPIO (October 23 to November 21) — The House of Legacies and Silence. Ruling planet is Mars. Lucky day is Tuesday. Lucky numbers are 3 and 7. Those born under the sign of the scorpion are lovers of books and knowledge, reserved, tenacious, determined, self-reliant, independent, and kind-hearted — and are also critical, suspicious, and grasping. They accumulate money easily, but sometimes become unscrupulous. They are clear, logical speakers, but can sound sarcastic. Smooth your rough edges by surrounding yourself with this gentle scent which will remind you to be less aggressive and domineering in your interactions with others.

SECRET OF VENUS — Usually known today only as the Goddess of Love, in Roman religion, The Goddess was the goddess of vegetation. In Imperial times she was worshipped as Venus Felix, bringer of good fortune, as Venus Victrix, bringer of victory, and as Venus Verticordia, protector of feminine chastity. Hence, the Secret of Venus Oil has legendary attributes which can bring you not only love, but good fortune, victory and chastity. Wear it any time you are weak and in need of assistance from the gods.

For those who wish to overcome an enemy who hates you without cause, make a protective talisman for yourself which will dissolve all hostility the foe may direct your way. On a small square of parchment, copy Verses 47 and 48 from Psalm 18, as given here:

It is God that avengeth me, and subdueth the
people under me.
He delivereth me from mine enemies:

Yea, thou liftest me up above those that rise up against

me: thou hast delivered me from the violent man.

Anoint the talisman with the Secret of Venus Oil weekly and carry it with you at all times.

SENSATION — A truly stimulating scent which can be used for many purposes. It reputedly brings encouragement to the depressed, passion to the frigid, hope to the discouraged, and reassurance to the defeated. Use in the daily bath or as a perfume.

SENSUALITY — Increase your sexual and erotic feelings when you make this your perfume of choice on special occasions.

Apply to the back of the knees, elbows, and around the neckline. Use sparingly as the fragrance is quite powerful.

SEPARATING — Two white candles, preferably jumbo sized ones, placed side by side, are used for this ritual which can be most effective in bringing discord, conflict, and descension into the relationship of two friends or lovers.

Place beneath each candle the name of one of the persons involved in your objective. This should be scribed with Dragon's Blood Ink onto a small square of parchment paper. Anoint the four corners of the talisman with the oil.

Anoint each candle also with the oil, beginning about two inches from the top, stroking downward.

Place the candles close together — but not touching — and burn for about ten minutes after which time extinguish the flames.

Each day thereafter, move the candles apart about an inch or two from the other and burn them for a few minutes. Repeat the ritual until the candles are exhausted or the relationship between those involved has completely disintegrated.

SEPARATION — When applied on the wrists and fingertips of two people, it causes them to detach their emotions from each other, thereby permitting them to part without undue stress or strain on the part of either person.

To get rid of anyone you wish to leave you alone, mix about one-half teaspoon of oil with a half cup of Four Thieves Vinegar. Stir it well daily, but let it set for three full days. At any time after the three days, sprinkle the mixture behind the back of the bothersome one as he or she leaves your home. This method is almost sure to cause them to quit visiting your house.

SESAME — Provides new hope when one is sick, discouraged, or lonely. If it is applied to the person, it leads to new paths of living, bringing perhaps a better job, interesting friendships, or an unexpected opportunity to travel.

To overcome melancholy, dress a large yellow candle with this oil and sprinkle it also over some Crucible of Courage Incense. Light both candle and incense and sit quietly, reading the entire Psalm 27, or these special verses given here:

> The Lord is my light and my salvation;
> whom shall I fear?
> The Lord is the strength of my life;
> of whom shall I be afraid?
> Though a host should encamp against me,
> my heart shall not fear;
> though war should rise against me,
> in this will I be confident.
> For in the time of trouble he shall hide me;
> he shall set me upon a rock.
> Wait on the Lord: be of good courage,
> and he shall strengthen thine heart:
> Wait, I say, on the Lord.

SEVEN AFRICAN POWERS (Seven Powers) — Make this your daily perfume and know that the Seven Saints — Chango, Elegua, Obatala, Ochun, Ogun, Orula, and Yemalla — will assist you in bringing to fruition you particular aims and desires.

> Chango helps with love and sexual problems.
> Elegua can increase one's personal powers.

Obatala specializes in money matters.
Ochun protects from all harmful influences.
Ogun can bring prophetic dreams.
Orula casts aside barriers in one's pathway.
Yemalla enhances one's chances for power
and success in life.

SEVEN CIRCLE — The symbolism of the number seven is well-known: the seven days of the week, the seven deadly sins, lucky seven, and many others, but this oil is associated with the Seven Gifts of the Holy Ghost — the gifts of wisdom, understanding, counsel, fortitude, knowledge, piety, and fear of the Lord. Use it prayerfully with the belief that all these gifts will be extended to your life.

SEVEN DAY UNCROSSING — Should you feel oppressed by a burden which has come upon you, free yourself within one week with a brief ritual each day for seven consecutive days.

Every morning, after your daily bath or shower, apply a few drops of oil around the ankles and wrists.

Use these daily affirmation given, repeating it three times:

1st day ... The dawn of freedom begins this day.

2nd day .. I clear the air with honesty and friendliness.

3rd day ... My faith in my self is steadfast.

4th day .. Today I take control of my own affairs.

5th day ... I am capable of making changes in my life.

6th day ... I fulfill my potential this very day.

7th day ... Today I am serene, at peace, and free!

Every day, for greater progress toward your goal, add this personal pledge to yourself: "Today I will not try to control others, nor will I allow others to control me."

SEVEN DROPS OF LOVE — Should a prospective new partner or lover cross your path, help matters progress quickly and successfully with this daily ritual for one full week. The beginning day is not important but, if a day is skipped at any point, the charm is broken. Quit the ritual and begin again after a full week has passed.

Place two candles side by side, but about ten or twelve inches apart, on a table or altar. With a nail or pin, scratch your name on one candle and the prospective lover's on the other. Rub the oil over the names on both candles.

Light the candles — yours first, the new lovers last. Let them burn for about ten minutes before extinguishing them for the day.

Repeat the ritual daily — at the same hour — and after the seventh day, bury whatever remains of the candles near the entrance to the home.

Before the next new moon, the object of your desires should be at your side.

SEVEN–ELEVEN — An unusual combination of the most popular lucky number together with the one which is most ominous to occultists. Hence, the blending can nullify the potential of any maleficent influences, hidden dangers, or planned treachery from others while, at the same time, drawing in the beneficial rays. Use as a perfume, or anoint the soles of the feet while dressing for the day.

SEVEN HOLY SPIRITS — This fragrance is dedicated to the seven Christian youths who, according to legend, hid in a cave about 250 AD to escape persecution for their faith — and fell asleep. It was 200 years later when they were discovered by accident and found to be miraculously preserved — awakening in their same youthful bodies as when they entered the refuge.

Perhaps this oil can remind one that, when in danger, retreat until the peril has faded. Then proceed with the objective, plan, or mission without hindrance from enemies.

SEVEN MEN — A strengthening oil — for body, soul, or spirit — which is applied to the forehead, nape of the neck, and soles of the feet.

Apply each morning after the bath. Within a few days, you should begin to feel more confident, forceful, and with great power and energy, both mentally and physically.

SEVEN POWERS — See Seven African Powers.

SEVENTH HEAVEN — When used on the body before engaging in sexual relations, it is said to bring satisfaction and gratification never before experienced.

To find out if one in whom you are interested is also interested in you, get a candle — pink if the object of the spell is a female, blue if male. Anoint the candle with the oil, light it and let it burn for at least ten minutes. Then snuff out the flame (do not blow as this will affect the results). If the dying smoke drifts in your direction, the person you desire is also interested in you, but if the smoke drifts away from you, the person is involved with another.

SHI SHI — Cleanse the home or work place of all obstacles in the path toward advancement, accomplishment, prosperity, and triumph over adversaries who may stand in one's way. Sprinkle a few drops of this commanding scent across entrance to the premises you wish to protect.

SHIFTING SANDS — If you are seeking a change, a separation, a turnabout in your situation, try this distinctive fragrance. If kept open in the home, it encourages a troublemaker to quietly and peacefully depart. If used as a perfume, it causes one to encounter new people, to have a chance at a better or different job, or to see an opportunity to move or travel.

To get rid of an unwanted lover, write the persistent one's name nine times on a square of parchment. Place the paper, with the side on which the name is written upwards, under a reversible candle (one which is black on the outside, red on the inside). Anoint the candle with the Shifting Sands Oil from bottom to top as you chant quickly nine times:

Leave me as softly as sands leave the shore,
Leave me as gently as we loved before.

Light the candle and let it burn out entirely. The rejected one will disappear from your life without any bitterness or anger.

SHOWERS OF GOLD — Used by those who need money in a hurry. Anoint coins or bills before spending them, and allegedly twice as many will return to the purse or pocket quickly.

SIETE MACHOS DROPS — For men only: wear it any time you are going out with your special lady, and you will be sure that you are her special man.

SNAKE — Helps to win the most difficult of court cases when rubbed on the hands before going into the courtroom.

When green candles are dressed with this and burned, it is said to help the sick recover.

To assure the solution to money problems, a green candle is anointed with this oil, and beneath the candle is placed a piece of parchment on which the petitioner has written the amount of money needed. For this spell to work, one must ask for one specific amount needed for a particular payment to settle one bill. Light the candle and let it burn until it is completely consumed.

The Snake Oil can also be used to bring suffering to an enemy. Make an image of the victim of heavy cardboard, or get a voodoo doll. Write the foe's name on the cardboard image, or securely attach a name tag to the doll. Soak the image overnight in the oil and then attach the image to a stick or rod of any kind which will not burn. Hold or hang the image over a burning fire. As the flames consume the image, repeat this curse:

> Dust to dust, fire to fire,
> You have provoked my ire.
> Suffer the pangs of remorse and sin,
> Know and feel the fix you're in.

SONG OF SOLOMON — On Solomon's ascension to the throne, Jehovah appeared to him and told him to choose a blessing. The young king, instead of asking for long life, riches, or success in war, prayed to be endowed with an understanding heart. His request was granted — and riches and honor were added also. In consequence of this endowment, Solomon was reputed to be wiser than all men. He became a philosopher and a poet — he spoke 3,000 proverbs, and 1,005 songs. If you wish to have the ability to speak or sing well, to understand better, and judge others justly, try this oil. Add it to incense, dress candles with it, or use as a perfume.

Solomon loved women as well as splendor. At one time his harem included 60 queens and 80 concubines. Over his lifetime his wives numbered 700 and his concubines totaled 300. Men who have worn this Song of Solomon Oil as their regular perfume have not claimed such results for themselves, but it is allegedly a highly magnetic fragrance which many women find impossible to resist.

SPANISH MOSS — Evil will not enter the home where this is used on the doorways. It may be rubbed around the door frame or sprinkled on the doormat. Use at least once every ten days to keep it active.

When there is a situation where it is believed that earthbound spirits, astral bodies, or evil spirits are tormenting or obsessing a person, these spirits can be freed and returned to the other world by the use of this oil. Make a conjure bag as a "home" for the spirits by placing in a red flannel or leather bag a few items which attract the dark beings — a turquoise stone, some Valerian Herb, and a photograph of the person who is afflicted. Into the bag pour one-half teaspoon of the Spanish Moss Oil. Place this bag in a small "bed" made of any small box which you have lined with Spanish Moss Herb. Cover the bag with a blanket of the moss and place it in a safe place in the home. So long as you keep the spirits well-fed by sprinkling the moss with the oil weekly, the person will not be troubled further.

SPEARMINT — A protective oil which keeps one's person and home safe from attack, danger, and intruders. For personal use, add to the bath or wear as a perfume. For home security, keep a few drops in an open bowl, adding several drops every week.

SPECIAL DICE — A special oil for those gamblers who need to win every time they play.

Use it in the bath or on the body.

To make your own personal lucky charm, draw a pair of dice on a square of parchment with Dove's Blood Ink. Write your name on the back of the paper, and place the talisman in a red flannel bag. Carry the bag in your pocket and anoint it with the oil just before going out to play. Touch it secretly when it's your turn to roll the dice.

If the racetrack is where you place your bets, use the above spell but draw a picture of a horseshoe on the parchment instead of the pair of dice. The other instructions remain the same except, of course, to touch the bag as you pick the horse and place your wager.

SPECIAL FAST LUCK — Clear away any stubborn resistance which may stand in the path of your aims or desires. Place a drop or two each morning at the entrance to your place of business or home so that all who enter will be favorably impressed with your plans or strategy for attaining your particular goals.

SPECIAL FAVOR — St. Jude, the saint of the impossible, may come to your aid when all other efforts have failed, if you try this oil rubbed on the temples just before retiring, along with this prayer. State your problem or request, and pray with faith:

> Grant me this favor if it be Thy will. I ask for this in humility and in complete faith in the goodness of God and his knowledge of what is best for me.

To get that much needed luck when things are truly desperate, get a talisman called the Serpent Seal, or Seal of Magic, which is from the Sixth and Seventh Books of Moses. It is a design which reputedly draws all the spirits to give magical assistance in bringing to the owner his need, desires, wishes, or requests. Write your special favor on the back of the paper seal, anoint all outer edges with the Special Favor Oil, and place it beneath a white Seven Knob Candle. Burn one knob of the candle each day for seven days and good fortune will almost surely arrive and linger in your life.

SPECIAL NO. 20 — Use this, one of the most potent of all the legendary occult oils, when going through a crisis, or when everyone and everything else seems to have failed you. Use nine drops in the daily bath for nine days, and after the bath apply to the instep of the foot, palms of the hands, and back of the neck at the hairline. Before the nine days is up, you should see a remarkable improvement in your condition.

If you feel that others are speaking against you and their tales are untrue or unjustified, wear the Special No. 20 Oil as your perfume daily so that no gossip can harm you and your reputation will remain untarnished.

SPELL BREAKING — Or Spell Breaker Oil. To protect oneself against spells being put upon you, use several drops in the bath once a week. If you feel a hex has already been placed against you, add the oil to the daily bath for seven consecutive days, chanting as you sprinkle it into the tub:

> I remove all the negative,

I am at peace with the world.
I break from all evil,
I am filled with love.

When you know the name of the foe who has placed a jinx on you, get a black doll and label it with the enemy's name. Place the doll in a small "coffin" (any empty small box will do) and sprinkle it with some dirt from a graveyard and a teaspoon of Valerian Herb. Then pour the Spell Breaking Oil over the doll, close the box quickly, and bury it after dark. Within a matter of days, the spell will have lost its power over you.

SPIKENARD — In the Bible, John 12, Verse 3 says, "Then took Mary a pound of ointment of spikenard, very costly, and anointed the feet of Jesus." And Mark 14, Verse 3 says, "...In the house of Simon the leper...came a woman having an alabaster box of ointment of spikenard, very precious, and she broke the box and poured it on his head." So symbolically Spikenard Oil means holiness. It is used to anoint the altar, to consecrate incense burners, to purify the premises in churches or the home, and to wear as a perfume to help one develop spiritually.

Spikenard retains its fragrance for centuries, and was one of the ingredients of the perfumes found in Tutankhamen's tomb when it was opened after about 5,000 years! Hence, its lingering scent is put to use by many who wear it when meeting with old acquaintances as they feel it brings back warm, fond memories from the past.

SPIRIT — This is of immense value when trying to contact beings from the other world, living or dead. Clairvoyants and mediums use it on wrists, throat, and forehead when attempting to see that which is beyond the human eyes' abilities.

To invoke the spirit of a particular person with whom you wish to give a message to or receive a communication from, obtain a black image candle in the form of a man or woman, depending upon the sex of the one with whom you are attempting to converse. Write the person's name on parchment paper with Eternal Black Ink and place it beneath the image candle. Anoint the image with the Spirit Oil and sprinkle it also on the edges of the name paper. Light the candle and invoke the spirit by saying:

> I conjure all the demons of the underworld, assembled
> here, to assist this spirit. Waken to my command,
> wherever you may be. Betake yourself and
> conjure up the spirit of (name of person).

Repeat the invocation three times, then sit quietly and listen for the spirit's entrance or a sound signaling his or her arrival. Then, speak softly your message or ask your question and wait for the reply. Many spirits are reluctant and do not appear at the first calling. If you get no results after about ten minutes wait, snuff out the candle. Wait at least another ten minutes, then light the candle again and invoke the spirit. If you fail after three attempts, wait until the next day before you try again.

SPIRIT GUIDE — This is used to advantage at seances, when using the Ouija Board, or any time one is attempting to contact other world beings.

Anoint the forehead, wrists, and ankles. Invite the spirits by lighting a white candle if the angelic spirits are those you wish as guests, a black one if those of the underworld are summoned. Chant this invitation seven times:

> Come, spirits, and be with us,
> We invite your presence here.
> Enter in peace and in peace depart.
> We welcome thee with love, not fear.

SPIRITUAL — Sometimes one's faith in God, other people, or one's own self can be shaken by circumstances not understood. When this happens, find a quiet hour and a comfortable place where you can sit and concentrate on the loss of confidence.

Rub the palms of the hands with the oil and read this inspiring prayer poem, "How To Be Happy," by an unknown author:

Are you almost disgusted with life, little man?
I'll tell you a wonderful trick
That will bring you contentment, if anything can.
Do something for somebody quick!
Are you awfully tired with play, little girl?
Wearied, discouraged, and sick —
I'll tell you the loveliest game in the world,
Do something for somebody, quick!
Though it rains, like the rain of the flood, little
   man,
And the clouds are forbidding and thick,
You can make the sun shine in your soul, little
   man
Do something for somebody, quick!
Though the stars are like brass overhead, little
   girl,
And the walks like a well-heated brick,
And our earthly affairs in a terrible whirl,
Do something for somebody, quick!

SPIRITUAL FAST LUCK — Anoint a green Seven Day candle with the fragrance. Light it as you pray this prayer, and be assured of good luck, good health, and good fortune in financial dealings for as long as the candle glows:

Most gracious God, I thank Thee for all
Thy blessings. Help me to keep my complete
faith in the goodness, and confidence in
the knowledge that my needs will be met
through my own efforts and thy bountiful
benevolence. Amen.

SPIRITUAL POWER — When one's faith fails and energy ebbs, the use of this fragrance can help regain confidence and vitality quickly.

Apply to the temples and back of the knees and meditate on this prayer of St. Francis of Assisi:

> Lord, make me an instrument of Thy peace;
> where there is hatred, let me sow love.
> where there is injury, pardon,
> where there is doubt, faith,
> where there is despair, hope,
> where there is darkness, light,
> where there is sadness, joy.
> O, Divine Master, grant that I may not so
> much seek to be consoled, as to console,
> to be understood, as to understand,
> to be loved, as to love,
> for it is in giving that we receive,
> it is in pardoning that we are pardoned,
> and it is in dying that we are born to eternal
> life.

SPRING FLOWERS — For those yearning for a new lease on life, this is the oil which may be the answer. Start using this exclusively as your perfume and see the uplifting and exhilarating effect it will have after just a few short weeks. It's practically a rejuvenation treatment in itself!

SPRING MINT — Sprinkle around a place of business to bring new customers and draw friendships your way.

SQUINT — It is alleged that if you put a little of this on a mate's clothes, he or she will not wander. If the partner is already gone, write a letter and anoint it with this bewitching love oil.

Combine this oil and a prayer to St. Martha for a powerful spell which should cause almost every straying lover to reconsider the decision to wander. First, secure a large green candle, anoint it with the Squint Oil (also called Squint Drops by some dealers) and dedicate the candle to St. Martha by repeating as you dress the candles:

St. Martha, I dedicate this candle to you

that you may grant my needs and help me conquer my difficulties. For you nothing is impossible, and I put my faith in you.

Beneath the candle place a piece of parchment on which you have written in Dove's Blood Ink the name of the one who has deserted you.

Light the candle and repeat this prayer:

I ask the intercession for my plea. Grant that (name of the lost love) will return to (your name) and that the time will be short between now and then. Until (name of the lost love) has returned, I ask that he (or she) suffer the aches I have suffered and that he (or she) is by my side again. I ask this in faith, for as you did conquer dragons and wild beasts, you can control (name of the lost love) and fulfill my request. In the name of justice and love, I ask this.

Amen.

Leave the candle burning for about fifteen minutes then extinguish it, repeating the ritual daily until the loved one has returned.

STAY AT HOME — Use in a mate's bath water, and on the soles of their shoes to keep a loved one from wandering.

Where there is discord in the home, burn some Peace Incense over which you have sprinkled the Stay at Home Oil. Tempers will quiet and tensions will dissolve when this ritual is followed weekly or as often as the situation requires.

STAY AWAY — Discourage visitors to the home by sprinkling a few drops across the threshold at all entrances. Should your mood change and you wish to have friends or relatives drop by, wash away the oil with the Helping Hand Wash.

STEADY WORK — Searching for a job is often a humiliating and depressing chore, but it is a necessity and the quicker and easier the chore is, the better chance of success.

Bolster your courage and confidence with a warm morning bath after which you apply a few drops of this poise building scent. Concentrate on the following verse from an unknown poet's poem titled, "Don't Quit":

> Success is failure turned inside out;
> The silver tint of the clouds of doubt.
> And you never can tell how close you are,
> It may be near when it seems afar;
> So stick to the fight when you're hardest hit;
> It's when things seem worst that you mustn't
> quit.

STRAWBERRY — A modern oil, becoming very popular when used as an attracting influence. Mix with incense, add to the bath, or use as a body oil, to draw fortunate circumstances in all areas of one's life.

SUCCESS — The Gods of Victory should smile on the one who rubs this oil on currency, coins, and money containers. Wear it as a perfume so that your undertakings in all areas of your life will thrive, flourish and bear fruit.

For success in business deals, carry in your pocket a red flannel bag containing a John the Conqueror Root, a Buckeye, and a Seal of Good Luck from the Sixth and Seventh Books of Moses. Each of these items should be anointed with the Success Oil before being placed in the bag and thereafter the bag itself in anointed.

For mastering a difficult situation you are facing, secure a Seven Knob Candle. If money is involved, choose a green color; if love or friendship is at stake, choose red; if trying to suppress one who is working against you, choose black.; if the objective is spiritual, choose white. Write the problem briefly on parchment paper and place it beneath the candle. Pour a few drops of the Success Oil on the top of the candle, light it, and burn until one knob is consumed. Then extinguish the candle until the next day. Continue the ritual for seven consecutive days, adding a few drops of the oil each day to the top of the candle just before lighting it. A solution to your dilemma, an answer to the problem, or a changed condition should develop before the candle is gone.

SUMMER RAIN — A perfume for all those emerging from "bad times." Its light fragrance lifts the spirits and softens sad memories so that one can face the future with assurance, confidence, and the knowledge that our higher power knows what is good for us even when we cannot understand his plan for us.

SUN — For as the sun is the creative, regenerative force in life, this fragrance is designed to enhance your naturally sunny personality so that all those who come in contact with you are restored and revived.

It is an oil for all those in creative work — writers, artists, musicians, dancers, actors, singers, designers, or builders.

From the Sixth and Seventh Books of Moses there is a Seal of the Sun, referred to by the many as the Seal of Honor and Wealth. This talisman is carried to attract plentiful gold, silver, and other of life's good blessings. Anoint the edges of the seal weekly with the Sun Oil.

SURE TO WIN — Rub on the hands before playing cards, dice, or roulette, or anoint one's bingo card, lottery ticket, or any other gambling paraphernalia to sway luck in your direction.

SWEET PEA — The user of this is drawn toward those strangers who may become friends or lovers. It attracts loyalty and affection when used daily on the wrists and forearms and behind the knees.

Make your own special talisman to draw love and attention from those around you by drawing on a piece of parchment in Dove's Blood Ink a triangle. Write your name three times, once on each side of the triangle. Inside the triangle draw a heart shape. Anoint the center of the heart with this oil and then place the talisman in a carrying case so that you will have it with you at all times. At least once a week remove the talisman from its case and anoint it with the Sweet Pea Oil.

T

TAME — Quiets and calms one's temper if applied to ear lobes, shoulders, or fingertips. Use it on an unruly child or one who is overwrought with emotional stress.

Rub on a lover to have them do your bidding without hesitation.

TANGERINE — Adds strength and go-power to all ritual incense and baths. Used to massage the body, it excites the senses and heightens one's sexual responses. Try it on a lazy lover.

TAURUS (April 21 to May 22) — Ruling planet is Venus. The House of Wealth and Industry. Lucky day is Friday. Lucky numbers are 2 and 7. Those born under the sign of the bull are determined, persistent, self-reliant, trustworthy, and have great physical and mental endurance powers. Many Tauruses have the capacity to become psychics, mediums, and faith healers, and your capacity to magnetize others can be enhanced by wearing this beguiling scent.

TEASING LOVER — When the romance sags and it needs a boost to help regain the freshness of its beginnings, try this rejuvenating scent.

Before your next encounter with your loved one, take a warm bath and add two heaping tablespoonsful of Love Bath Crystals (or salts if you prefer). After the bath, apply the oil to the shoulders. Greet your date with a smile and a kiss. The magic should return to the relationship with no further delay.

TEMPLE — A sacred oil used by mediums and spiritualists to develop power. Apply to the crown of the head, all around the neckline, and on the hands.

Used by all who meditate to clear the mind of extraneous thoughts so that, free from all external influences, our innate wisdom can manifest itself and function to its fullest possibilities.

TEMPTATION — To keep a lover from being tempted by others, cut a small heart shape from a piece of red cloth. Soak the heart in the oil for two full days. Then remove it from the oil and let it dry. Sew or pin it onto the lover's underpants. Anoint the heart with oil regularly, whenever you feel your loved one may be susceptible to temptation, or at least once a week.

If you feel tempted and wish to resist another's advances, fortify your good intentions by using the oil in your bath or as a perfume when you leave home.

TEN COMMANDMENTS — One of the holy oils used for anointing sacred tools, incense burners, altars, and such.

For those sorely troubled by past mistakes or regrets for opportunities passed by, it does one well to remember that the lowest ebb comes just as the tide is turning. Don't let the good life pass you by — and it surely will if time is wasted by grieving about yesterday's losses or disappointments. Use the oil on the wrists and temples, and pray with faith this prayer by an unknown author:

> God, make me brave for life; oh, braver than
> this.
> Let me straighten after pain,
> As a tree straightens after rain,
> Shining and lovely again.
> God, make me brave for life; much braver than

this.
As the blown grass lifts, let me rise
From sorrow with quiet eyes,
Knowing Thy way is wise.
God, make me brave,
Life brings such blinding things.
Help me to keep my sight;
Help me to see aright,
That out of dark comes light.

THREE JACKS & KING — Sometimes offered as simply Three Jacks Oil or as Three Knaves Oil. New Orleans gamblers swear this is the luckiest of all the good luck oils. They rub it on their hands before opening the deck.

For success in settling a court case, use the oil, a Galengal Root, three Red Cross Candles, and some John the Conqueror Incense. For one week before your court date, perform the ritual in this manner. On the first day, place your galengal root in a bottle of Three Jacks & King Oil and let it remain there all week. On the second day, anoint a Red Cross Candle with the oil and burn it while you read Psalm 20. On the third day, add a few drops of the oil to some John the Conqueror Incense and burn it. Read the Psalm 20 while it burns. On the fourth day, anoint the second Red Candle with the oil, light it and read Psalm 20. On the fifth day, repeat this ritual with the John the Conqueror Incense. On the sixth day, repeat the ritual using the third Red Cross Candle. On the seventh day, take the Galengal Root with you into court, and the scales of justice will surely be weighted in your favor.

THREE KINGS — According to tradition, Kaspar, Melchior, and Balthasar were the three magi (or wise men or kings) who brought the infant Jesus gifts of gold, frankincense, and myrrh.

Many talents, endowments, and favors may come to those who use this perfume. Apply it to the temples for wisdom, to the throat so that you speak only kindly and with truth, and at the wrists so that the hands will be helpful to those in need.

THRIFTY — Should you require the generosity of friends, relatives, or complete strangers, their willingness to part with their money can be increased if this oil is rubbed surreptitiously onto the back of their hands.

It can also be employed to aid you in conserving the funds you have. Anoint the corners of each bill in your possession with the oil and chant as you do so:

Bless this cash I have to spend,
Let me use it with utmost care.
If I use it well, it will not end,
For more will replace it is my prayer.

TIBET — See Queen of Tibet Oil.

TIBETAN — A portion of the Buddhist Creed has been translated by Csoma to this simple verse:

No vice is to be committed;
Every virtue must be perfectly practiced;
The mind must be brought under entire subjection;
This is the commandment of Buddha.

Whether Buddhist, Christian, Jewish, or humanist, the substance seems to be a goal for all to attain. Anoint the forehead with the oil while one meditates upon the objectives of the Buddhist, or one's own religious faith.

TIGER — This allegedly turns pussycats into aggressive beasts. It is not confined to lovers, but assists one in all business and personal relationships.

To overpower another's objections to your plans, add nine drops of the oil to Domination Incense and burn it as you explain your idea to the person you wish to support you in this objective, and all their defenses against you will be shattered.

TIME — When the pressures come, anoint the forehead, wrists, and forearms with this oil and sit quietly for fifteen minutes. A solution is likely to emerge.

In a time of grief or temptation, a time of sorrow or trouble, know in your heart that there is a purpose for all things, even when we cannot see or understand it. Sit quietly as you apply the oil to the throat, arms, and palms. Then read the following Bible passage, Ecclesiastes 3, Verses 1 through 8. Read this over and over until the message has filled your entire being, and tranquility and peace have come upon you.

> To every thing there is a season,
> and a time to every purpose under the heaven;
> A time to be born, and a time to die,
> A time to plant,
> and a time to pluck up that which is planted;
> A time to kill, and a time to heal;
> A time to break down, and a time to build up;
> A time to weep, and a time to laugh;
> A time to mourn, and a time to dance;
> A time to cast away stones,
> and a time to gather stones together;
> A time to embrace,
> and a time to refrain from embracing;
> A time to get, and a time to lose;
> A time to keep, and a time to cast away;
> A time to read, and a time to sew;
> A time to keep silence, and a time to speak;
> A time to love, and a time to hate;
> A time of war, and a time of peace.

TOUCH ME NOT — Should you desire not to be approached by those you do not care for, and yet on occasion, circumstances require that your paths cross, add this to the bath water, or rub it on the body after a shower, as you chant:

> (Name), (Name), I do not wish to see,
> (Name), (Name), Stay far away from me.
> I wish you no harm, no tragic fate,
> I beg only that our paths do not integrate.

Chances are that you will be spared a face to face confrontation with the one you wish to avoid.

TRANQUIL — François de Salignac de La Mothe Fenelon, late 16th Century theologian and writer, wrote, "Peace does not dwell in outward things, but within the soul; we may preserve it in the midst of the bitterest pain, if our will remain firm and submissive. Peace in this life springs from acquiescence, not in the exemption from suffering."

And this soothing, relaxing oil, when applied to the forehead and temples can ease tension, strain, and rigidity. This relaxation allows the mind to dismiss disturbing thoughts so that clear, orderly thinking can prevail and a solution or resolution of the problem can enter into the mind's reflections.

TRANQUILITY — Similar to Tranquil, it clears the mind of extraneous thoughts so that the matter at hand can be considered clearly and sensibly. In this way an intelligent decision can be arrived at which will be the most advantageous and the least harmful to all concerned.

TRINITY — For love, luck, and longevity, use this. Occult practitioners and mediums use it whenever they meditate, pray, or attempt any psychic work.

To provide yourself with an impregnable defense against evil, get a Seal of Jesus of God design, taken from the Sixth and Seventh Books of Moses. Anoint it with the Trinity Oil as you repeat these words from the seal, "The innocent, holy blood of Jesus Christ, the Son of God, cleanses us from all sin and give you the spirits of eternal rest and peace. Therefore, may the spirits of Jesus Christ redeem you from all pain and suffering, and give us the treasures that are here. Amen."

Carry the seal with you always, keeping it in a suitable case so that it does not come to harm, and repeat the anointing and affirmation weekly.

TRIPLE ACTION — Wear this as one's personal perfume as it is composed of elements which attract the three most important things in life: love, health, riches.

Write your special wish or requirement on a square of parchment paper with Dove's Blood Ink. Anoint the edges of the paper with the oil as you chant three times this affirmation:

> I nurture my body with exercise, a good diet, and adequate sleep.
> My love goes out to others, and is returned threefold.
> My riches are my friends, my family and my serenity.

TRIPLE CROSS — Use this as a perfume when you are among persons whose motives you do not trust. It protects one from devious schemes — whether devised by friends, strangers, or known enemies.

It can also be sprinkled across the threshold of your home, or applied to the door handles of your car, to shield the premises from malicious mischief makers.

TRIUMPH — To insure a prosperous, successful, and personally satisfying day, use this after the morning bath.

Apply to the soles of the feet and backs of the hands so that, wherever you wander, you will be greeted with an opportunity for enrichments, and whatever your hands touch will be blessed with an uplifting and enlightening reward.

TUBEROSE — The tuberose was known to the Malayans as "Mistress of the Night", and there is an old tradition that the most virtuous of women will succumb to the exotic influence of the tuberose's seductive breath. So men wear it to entice women who have not shown any interest in their advances. Women who wish to excite men also wear it.

To those under strain, it helps bring serenity and peace of mind when used in the bath water, and calms the nerves of those who are agitated.

TURN BACK — When a stubborn harmful situation continues to bother you and your home, cleanse the premises thoroughly with the Van Van Wash (about a half-cupful to a half gallon of water). Immediately after the cleaning, rub a few drops of oil on each windowsill, and at each entrance. As you apply the fragrance, at each anointing point read this protective promise from Psalm 18, Verses 1 through 3:

> I will love thee, O Lord, my strength.
> The Lord is my rock, and my fortress,
> and my deliverer; my God, my strength,
> in whom I will trust; my buckler,
> and the horn of my salvation,
> and my high tower.
> I will call upon the Lord,
> who is worthy to be praised;
> so shall I be saved from mine enemies.

To insure this continued protection, repeat the cleansing ritual once a week.

TURTLE — Protects one from accidents so that a full, long life is assured. Wear it as a perfume and use it weekly in the bath.

TUTTI FRUITI — A spicy mixture which gives a lift wherever it is used. Apply to light bulbs, add to bath, use as a perfume, or rub on another person. Brings vitality, vivacity, and virility!

TWELVE APOSTLES — Should your troubles seem overwhelming, and no path out of the turmoil can be envisioned, anoint the forehead with the oil and sit quietly as you pray this 19th Century prayer:

> Faint not nor fear, for help is here.
> The twelve Jesus chose will be ever near.
> Cast care aside, boundless mercy will provide.
> There is naught to fear with these at my side.

Tranquility and release from tension will envelop the body, mind, and spirit.

U

UNBINDING — Loose the chains which prevent you from achieving your full potential.

If there is a specific goal you are attempting to reach, write your objective in a few words on the reverse of a Seal of Jesus of God from the Sixth & Seventh Books of Moses. Place it beneath a large brown candle. Burn for about ten minutes daily until all hindrances are withdrawn from your pathway to success.

UNCROSSING — To remove all types of hexes, curses, and crossed conditions, add nine drops to the bath water for nine consecutive days.

To rid the home of evil influences, add nine drops to a cup of water and sprinkle about the premises each morning for nine consecutive days.

UNFAITHFUL — If a lover is behaving differently than usual, and you suspect that infidelity is the reason for the change, rub the oil over the soles of the loved one's feet. This can be done secretly while the lover is sleeping, or as a massage at any time. Once the oil is applied, the straying one will not be interested in or able to have intimate relations with others.

UNHEXING — Very similar to Jinx Removing.

Apply to the temples and neckline at bedtime. Close the eyes and pray this prayer of Pope Gregory the Great until peaceful, refreshing sleep comes:

Dear Jesus, Savior of the world,

Our Savior be today,
Protect our hearts in darkness hurled,
And guide us in thy way.
Amen.

URANUS — Uranus, the son of Gaea, the Greek goddess of the earth, used to hide his children from the light in the hollows of the earth. If you wish to hide anything — particularly secret information — write and secret on parchment which you have soaked in this oil and then dried. Burn the paper in the flame of a green candle. The secret will never be discovered unless you yourself reveal it.

Uranus rules the fields of science and invention, and most of those born during the times when Uranus is the ruling planet are apt to be ahead of most others in discovering new things. They pioneer ideas and inventions which can bring about changes in industry, society, and in government. Use the oil to inspire your natural talents, and to become more open in your relations with others, as Uranians are usually a bit eccentric and have some trouble in developing friendships and sustaining love affairs.

VAN VAN — Many, many uses. Anoint charms, seals, or talismans with it to increase their powers. Dress candles with it for more potency, particularly the Seven-Knob Wishing Candles under which you have placed your secret desire written on parchment paper.

When worn on the arms and shoulders, the oil attracts interest and love.

For uncrossing, use seven drops in the bath daily for seven consecutive days.

VANILLA — One of the newer occult oils, recommended as an additive to one's floor wash to bring happy occasions to the premises. It is also used on the person as a perfume.

For continuing good fortune in one's life, carry two tonka beans in a small bag and anoint the bag with the oil once a week.

VENUS — Use to form friendships, attract love, obtain grace and honors, force others to come to you, and to be admired by friends and strangers alike. This oil is said to make one irresistible when worn as a perfume.

Sprinkle over Lovers Incense and form an "inescapable trap" by burning it when the one you desire is in the room.

The planet Venus rules love affairs and governs musical arts and dancing. Those who love beautiful clothes and erotic pleasures use this fragrance to attract those things.

VERBENA — To remove all curses placed upon you, or as a protection against any hex attempted against you, first take a warm bath to which you have added about two tablespoonsful of the Dragon's Blood Bath. Soak in the tub for fifteen minutes. Dry yourself, and use the oil as a body rub. Do this once a week for constant protection from witchcraft or black magic.

VETIVERT — Overcomes any spell which may be placed upon one. Apply five drops to Dragon's Blood Incense and burn to dispel evil forces.

To place a curse on a foe, get a candle made in the shape of a skull. Write the name of the enemy on the back of the candle by using a nail, a thin knife, heavy wire, or any sharp object which will carve the candle. Pour the oil over the skull and light it, chanting this curse:

> (name of enemy), twist and turn, squirm like a worm,
> Live with pain and rain, nobody to care.
> Heart will churn, bones ache, and heart burn.

VIBRATION — This is a very expensive, very potent love oil which is usually made to order individually for a person who is seeking to capture a particular partner. It is believed to set up intense rays of sensual currents between the two lovers. Apply to both bodies.

VICTORY — Should one become engaged in a contest of wills with an adversary, triumph will be yours if this fragrance is applied daily to the earlobes, fingertips, and heels. When the occasion to express your point of view arises, present your version of the problem calmly and in an orderly manner — stressing the positive features of your position — without hostility or bitterness against your opponent.

VICTORY OVER EVIL — Wear as your daily perfume to be assured of protection from all sinister plots, fraudulent schemes, spiteful gossip, or harmful tricks which may be planned by adversaries.

    As you apply the shielding fragrance, recite Verses 10 and 11 from Psalm 91:

> No evil will befall you,
> Nor will any plague come near your tent.
> For He will give His angels charge concerning
>   you,
> To guard you in all your ways.

VIOLET — Violets are attributed to the goddess of love, and symbolize modesty and is also the occult symbol of twilight.

    Use five drops in the bath water daily as an aid toward marital peace and happiness.

    When rubbed over the stomach, it can alleviate pain in that area.

    To receive information through dreams or visions, secure a Seal of Knowledge from the Sixth and Seventh Books of Moses. Anoint the edges of the paper with the Violet Oil and place the seal beneath the pillow before retiring for the night.

This ritual, if done nightly, will cause all dreams to be much clearer and easier to understand.

VIRGO (August 23 to September 22) — Ruling planet is Mercury. House of Health and Service. Lucky day is Wednesday. Lucky numbers are 7 and 9. Typical characteristics of those born under this sign are modesty, unselfishness, an industrious nature, and pleasing personality. They are very active, have good endurance, and an ardent love nature. Best professions for Virgos are author, musician, doctor, or lawyer. They often put too much faith in the truthfulness and trustworthiness of others. This scent will bolster their sometimes easily hurt feelings and damaged ego, and help them maintain continued health, happiness, and peace of mind.

VIRGIN OLIVE — The holiest of the sacred oils. It is never used as a perfume, but to cleanse and purify altars, incense burners, talismans, charms, and any other hallowed implements.

VISION — Said to bring prophetic dreams when applied to the forehead and temples just before retiring.

Used by spiritualists when calling upon the spirits for messages or guidance. A simple Prayer of Conjuration follows:

I conjure thee by the authority of God, the father almighty,
by the virtue of heaven and the sins of hell,
by the power of the elements, the stones,
the plants, and the animals,
I conjure thee to come into my presence,
Come at once and fulfill my petition.

The Conjuration is repeated four times, once in each direction — north, south, east, and westerly. When the spirit appears, he is commanded in this manner:

I speak to thee clearly. I command thee to do my bidding forthwith.

The spiritualist or magician then tells the spirit his request — simply, explicitly, and exactly. The spirit is then dismissed by saying:

> O Spirit, Thou may now leave to do my bidding.
> Leave without harm to any man or beast.
> Leave in peace and quiet.
> Leave, and be at my disposal when I call thee again.
> May there be peace between thee and me forever.

VOODOO — A Haitian crossing oil. To destroy an enemy's powers, write the foe's name nine times on parchment. Anoint the paper with nine drops of the oil. Then burn the paper in the flame of a black candle and bury the ashes.

To cause distress to an enemy, add some of the Voodoo Oil to Black Arts Incense and mix well. Write the foe's name on parchment, anoint it with the oil, and place the paper beneath the incense. Burn the incense and paper, and sprinkle the ashes in front of your enemy's door after midnight.

To find out if someone is speaking the truth, place beneath his or her chair or mattress a Bible into which you placed a piece of parchment on which you have drawn a cross (not an X, but a cross of the shape of the one on which Jesus was crucified). Anoint the edges of the paper with the Voodoo Oil. If the person has lied to you, he or she will become sick after sitting on the chair or sleeping on the bed.

WALL BREAKER — Do not let frustrations with barriers which have come between you and your progress toward the goal you have set for yourself cause you to surrender and give up.

Obstacles and impediments can be removed quickly by anointing the inside of the elbows, back of the knees, neck, and ears. Then read and concentrate on the message in this powerful short poem by an unknown author:

> Through this toilsome world, alas!
> Once and only once I pass;
> If a kindness I may show,
> If a good deed I may do
> To a suffering fellow man,
> Let me do it while I can.
> No delay, for it is plain
> I shall not pass this way again.

WAR — This is generally utilized to create tranquility and peace out of chaotic situations. When you feel that another person is taking advantage of you, slandering you to others, or in general making your life a constant conflict, it is time to replace pandemonium and confusion with tranquility and order.

Each morning, after the daily shower or bath, anoint the throat with the fragrance, chanting as you dress:

> This is a day of peace,
> Calm, quiet, senses keen.
> This is a day of joy,
> Love to share, heart serene.

WEALTHY WAY — Worn to attract riches — especially when worn to bingo games, the race track, or while indulging in any games of chance.

To receive a financial blessing, secure two jumbo candles — one green and one white. Anoint the green candle with the Wealthy Way Oil and the white candle with your own special Astrological Oil (or Zodiac Oil if you cannot obtain quickly the particular oil for your birthdate). Place the two candles on a table about twelve to eighteen inches apart. Beneath the white candle place a parchment paper with your name written on it in Dove's Blood Ink. Beneath the green candle place a dollar bill and a piece of parchment on which you have written with the same Dove's Blood Ink the exact amount of money you need for a particular purpose. Light both candles, the green first and then the white, and burn them for ten minutes, all the while sitting and concentrating on the objective you need to achieve with the ritual. After ten minutes extinguish the two candles. On the second day, repeat the ritual after you have moved the green candle two or three inches closer to the white candle. The ritual is continued for seven days, each day moving the green candle closer to the white one which remains in its original position. If the entire amount of money is not received by the end of one week, wait for a full week before the spell is repeated.

WEED OF MISFORTUNE — Used to change one's luck from bad to more fortunate. Discontinue as soon as things pick up.

To help bring good fortune into your life, secure a Grand Symbol of Solomon Seal, anoint the edges of it with the oil and place it beneath some Frankincense Incense onto which you have sprinkled the Weed of Misfortune Oil. Light the incense in the morning when you arise, and read Psalm 46. Do this each day, adding a bit of incense and a few drops of oil daily.

WHITE ROSE — For inner peace and serenity, use this fragrance as a daily perfume. For a peaceful home, dress a white candle with the oil and as you light it, repeat this short prayer:

> God, grant me the serenity to accept the
> things I cannot change,
> The courage to change the things I can,
> And the wisdom to know the difference.

To gain personal and spiritual strength during times of stress, place a packet of dried rose buds or petals in a small open bowl. Sprinkle nine drops of the White Rose Oil over the flowers each morning upon arising, and recite the 23rd Psalm. At sunset each evening, take the bowl outside and blow a few petals in each direction — east, west, north, and south. Replenish the rose buds from time to time as necessary. The required strength and courage will surely come to the one who follows this ritual.

WILL POWER — This oil, applied to the various parts of the body just after the bath, will add that extra strength needed from time to time.

Apply to the throat for the courage to say the words you need to say, or for the restraint to keep the tongue still when the situation is not in you favor.

Add a few drops to a pan of water and soak the feet in it if you must make a trip which you are dreading. The journey will be made safe and enjoyable.

For weight loss, apply to the stomach before the meal to help assuage the pangs of hunger, thereby assisting one to cut down the intake of food.

WINNER'S CIRCLE — Sometimes called simply Winner's Oil. It has been said that, when there is only one winner in a game of cards, that one is the one who wears the Winner's Circle Oil!

When good luck evades you, secure a Seal of Spirits from the Sixth and Seventh Books of Moses. On the back of the seal, in the Dove's Blood Ink, write these ten names of God.

1. Eheia
2. Jod
3. Tetragrammaton Elohim
4. El
5. Elohim Gibor
6. Eloha
7. Adonai Sabaoth
8. Elohim Sabaoth
9. Sadai
10. Adonai Melech

Anoint all edges of the seal with the Winner's Circle Oil and place it in a carrying case so that the seal is protected. Place this case in the pocket, or pin it to the underclothes so that the seal is with you at all times. It can bring quick service and help in all things.

WINNING NUMBER — Anoint your lottery tickets, racing selections, bingo cards, etc., with this potent gambling oil. As the oil is applied, chant three times quickly:

> I wonder if the number will be,
> Zero, one, two, three, or four.
> In my mind's eye, let me see,
> Five, six, seven, eight, or nine,
> Which ones bring good luck to me.

As various numbers come to mind, note them and place your wagers on those you feel will be the most auspicious ones.

WINTERGREEN — Use a few drops in the bath water to keep or induce good health, or add to the wash water to prevent disease and illness in the home.

WISDOM — Charles Hamilton Aide, 19th Century poet, wrote:

> I sit beside my lonely fire
> And pray for wisdom yet;
> For calmness to remember
> Or courage to forget.

There is much perception and discernment in this short verse, and should you have a conflict over whether to hold onto hurtful things, or to dismiss them and surge ahead toward a serene future, write you dilemma on a small square of parchment and place the token beneath a white candle.

Anoint the candle, from the top downward, with the oil for knowledge. Light the flame and, before the candle has burned completely, the solution to your quandary will have become clear.

WISHING — Usually the same as Mojo Oil, this is often used with Seven-Knob Candles. Anoint the candle with the oil before it is lighted. Write your wish on parchment paper with Dove's Blood Ink and place it under the candle. Burn one knob of the candle each day, concentrating on your wish. Repeat for seven consecutive days.

WISTERIA — Occultists, metaphysicians, healers, and voodooists alike all praise this oil. When worn as a perfume it attracts good vibrations. Sprinkle it on the floor to draw happy occasions to the premises.

To make better things come into your life, combine in your incense burner equal amounts of Wisteria and Double Action Incense. Sprinkle on the incense several drops of the Wisteria Oil, light it, and burn for about fifteen minutes daily. Each evening add several drops of the oil to your warm bath, and wear the oil as a perfume when you go out.

WITCH'S — Sometimes called Witch's Formula Oil. There are many and varied uses of this ancient concoction. It is used to get rid of interfering people who are causing trouble. Place a bit of the hair of the mischief-maker in a bottle of this and let it soak for seven days. On the eighth day, remove the hair from the bottle and place it on top of some Domination Incense. Burn the incense and toss the ash out into the wind. That troublemaker will no longer be a menace to you or to your home.

To cause discord and unrest between persons who have been disloyal to you, make a Table of Mars. This is a square of 5, numbers 1 to 25. Each column totals 65, and the total of all is 325.

11	24	7	20	3
4	12	25	8	16
17	5	13	21	9
10	18	1	14	22
23	6	19	2	15

Use the Dragon's Blood Ink to make this square on parchment paper. On the back of the seal, write the name of those you wish to suffer remorse and regret for the harm they have done to you. Place the seal beneath some Lucifer Incense. Light the incense and leave the room at once. After the incense is burned out, take the ashes which are left in the burner and bury them in the ground.

WOLF'S EYE — A protective scent which forms an aura of security wherever this is used.

Sprinkle it in the home at entrances and on windowsills so that burglars cannot gain entry.

Anoint the feet so that one's steps will be directed along a safe path wherever one ventures.

WORMWOOD — This is one of the black arts oils, and is usually used on those who have made you suffer, either by their actions or by their neglect. The method of use depends upon circumstances. It can be added to the enemy's bath, and this is usually very effective, as it draws back all the mean and ugly vibrations which have been put out by that person.

If you cannot reach the enemy directly, go away from your own home and sprinkle the oil in a large X shape on the ground. Say the name of the enemy and repeat three times as you sprinkle:

> Turn, worm, turn quick,
> and crawl far, far away from me.
> Squirm, worm, squirm,
> Find the home where you ought to be.

When there is a person in your life with whom you have been intimately involved, and the time has come when you wish to discontinue the relationship, but the other person does not seem ready to let you go, use the Wormwood Oil in any one or several of these ways: add a few drops to the water in which you wash the ex-lover's clothes; sprinkle the oil in their shoes; secure some of the unwanted one's hair and nail clippings and boil them in a cup of water to which you have added some of the oil, then dig a hole in the ground and pour the mixture into it, recovering the hole with dirt and packing it down firmly; or write a letter to the one you wish to leave your life (the content of the message does not have to be on this subject at all) and anoint your writing paper with the oil.

𝒳

XX DOUBLE CROSS — This powerful oil can protect your home from double-dealing and deceitful enemies. Sprinkle it across the threshold every seventh day — preferably on Wednesdays as this is the day of theft and deceit.

Also see Double Cross listing.

X Y Z — A three purpose blend which brings those extra benefits, youthful thoughts and feelings, and zest of life into your daily living.

This is also what is sometimes called an oil of gratitude. It is used when a problem has been solved, a solution has been found, a situation has improved, or a barrier has been removed. Anoint the hands and neckline with the oil, and repeat with sincerity the Psalm 95, Verses 1 through 6:

O come, let us sing unto the Lord;
Let us make a joyful noise to the rock
of our salvation.
Let us come before his presence with thanksgiving,
and make a joyful noise unto him with psalms.
For the Lord is a great God,
and a great King above all gods.
In his hand are the deep places of the earth;
the strength of the hills is his also.
The sea is his, and he made it;
and his hands formed the dry land.
O come, let us worship and bow down;
let us kneel before the Lord our maker.

The one who follows this ritual at appropriate times will

almost certainly have many added blessings flow into their life.

Y

YLANG YLANG — An attracting oil primarily used to draw attention to oneself, but it is also of value when used while seeking employment, and to soothe a troubled marriage. For a peaceful home, add to the bath water or apply directly to the body of both partners.

YULA — A Chinese formula originating from a native flowering tree with large, brilliant, snow-white blossoms.

According to legend, the fragrance — when used by an unwed woman — will bring a proposal before the year is gone.

YUZA YUZA — A fragrance from the Japanese which has a reputation for settling quarrels between two antagonists.

Apply a few drops on a letter of conciliation which one party sends to another and the disagreement will be soon resolved to the satisfaction of both parties.

Z

ZODIAC OIL — This is generally a mixture of all the astrological fragrances and is used as a perfume, or in the bath water, to attract favorable planetary vibrations at any time.

Under Astrological Oils the twelve zodiacal signs and their dates are listed for those who wish to use their specific blend. If one does not know their exact birthdate, the Zodiac Oil will serve them nicely.

ZORBA — Of unknown origin, this is a sensual formula which reputedly heightens the sexual senses of those who have considered themselves frigid or abnormally adverse to sexual intercourse. Apply the oil to the temples, back of the neck, and inner thighs.

ZULA ZULA — A hexing oil, used in spells designed to get revenge, or to bring harm or even death to an enemy. Use with caution.

A potent spell is affected when one makes an image of the foe of melted wax to which nine drops of the oil has been added. Mold a human figure of the wax as it hardens and place the image on a piece of black cloth. With a heavy needle of other sharp object, scratch the enemy's name onto the doll. Then wrap the black cloth around the doll and put it away for a full day. After that time, each day for nine consecutive days, take the doll out and sprinkle it with nine more drops of the oil and stick a needle or pin into the image as you chant:

> May each pin I stick in your heart,
> Hurt you as you've hurt me.
> I stab you well, I wish you hell,
> Cry, sigh, die, one, two, three.

INTERNATIONAL IMPORTS
PUBLISHER & DISTRIBUTOR OF NEW AGE BOOKS
BOOKS IN PRINT

Are You Mediumistic?	1.95
Black & White Magic - Marie Laveau	4.95
Candle Burning Magic - Anna Riva	4.95
Crystal Gazing (Six Lessons) - Ra Mayne	2.95
Devotions to the Saints - Anna Riva	4.95
Domination - Anna Riva	4.95
Golden Secrets of Mystic Oils - Anna Riva	5.95
How To Conduct a Seance - Revised by Anna Riva	2.95
How to Use a Ouija Board - St. Christopher	5.95
Magic with Incense & Powders - Anna Riva	4.95
Modern Herbal Spellbook - Anna Riva	4.95
Modern Witchcraft Spellbook - Anna Riva	4.95
Old Love Charms & Spells - Tarostar & Briten	5.95
Powers of the Psalms - Anna Riva	4.95
Prayer Book - Anna Riva	4.95
Secrets of Magical Seals - Anna Riva	4.95
Spellcraft, Hexcraft & Witchcraft - Anna Riva	4.95
Voodoo Handbook of Cult Secrets - Anna Riva	4.95
Witch's Spellcraft - Tarostar	6.95
Your Lucky Number, Forever - Anna Riva	5.95

You can visit our website www.indioproducts.com

Ask for these books at a new age bookstore, occult supply store or botanica. You can also order from us. Check the boxes next to the books you have selected and add the total. Shipping costs are $1.50 for the first book and $ .50 for each additional book. California residents add 8.25% for sales tax. Sorry, no COD's. Foreign customers shipping costs $4.00 for the first book and $ .50 for each additional book.

SEND ORDER TO:

INTERNATIONAL IMPORTS
236 W. MANCHESTER AVE.
LOS ANGELES, CA 90003

NAME _____

ADDRESS _____

CITY _____ STATE _____ ZIP _____
